Dear
Queer Self

Dear Queer Self

An Experiment in Memoir

Jonathan Alexander

ACRE

CINCINNATI 2022

Acre Books is made possible by the support of the Robert and Adele Schiff Foundation and the Department of English at the University of Cincinnati.

ISBN-13 (pbk) 978-1-946724-46-5
ISBN-13 (e-book) 978-1-946724-47-2

Designed by Barbara Neely Bourgoyne
Cover art by Jonathan Alexander

The press is based at the University of Cincinnati, Department of English and Comparative Literature, McMicken Hall, Room 248, PO Box 210069, Cincinnati, OH, 45221–0069.

Acre Books books may be purchased at a discount for educational use. For information please email business@acre-books.com.

For all of those with whom I saw the decade in. . . .

Dear
Queer Self

Preface

I suppose I mean those things worth having when all the dust has—
when all *my* dust has settled.
I close my eyes and try and imagine them.
—Samuel Beckett, *Krapp's Last Tape*

In 2017 I published a small book, *Creep: A Life, a Theory, an Apology*, which I called a "critical memoir." *Creep* combined personal narrative, theoretical musings, and some cultural analysis of books and movies to convey my deep sense of my own, in a word, *creepiness*. As a really shy and nerdish boy in the Deep South in the '70s and '80s, a boy everyone thought would grow up to be queer, and who admittedly had many queer feelings, I learned early and often that such feelings made me a creep. Having a distant and emotionally cold father didn't help. Nor did my looks. Tall but slight, I was cross-eyed, gangly, uncoordinated, and a little femme; my appearance alone unsettled the good conservative Christians and Catholics that surrounded me. While I could try to butch up my mannerisms, there was only so much a boy could change about his looks. As for my feelings, my very queer feelings about other boys, I swore that I would do everything in my power to change *them*. I would *not* be queer. I would *not* be the faggot that I seemed destined to be, that everyone thought I already was. I failed, for which I am grateful. But along the

1

way to that failure, I developed a sense that I was a lurking menace, both to others and to myself. A menace to my own soul.

I'm largely over that sense of "negative" creepiness, and I delight in the creepiness that remains behind. While writing *Creep* was therapeutic, even purgative in some ways, I have worried in retrospect that it too easily imposes a schema on the capacious messiness of a life story, or at least part of a life story, that refuses (and don't they all?) the abstract tidiness of theory. I am not, after all, really a creep. But what am I? And how does one answer that question when one has an equal desire, in the thick of a life still unfolding, to refuse to answer it? Perhaps another way to put this: Is it possible to write about my past pain and difficulty but also honor the path, the trajectory, that often did not seem to have a fixed destination—that, frankly, still doesn't?

So, *Dear Queer Self* is an experiment in memoir, an attempt to tell the story—and this time, more of it—in such a way that it circles and circles around the still beating hearts of the matter, just as memory does. Our historical sense of ourselves is always given through the pressures of the present, the promises of the future, the lingering past, all circles within circles, around and around we go, there and back again. Hence my use throughout of the second person, addressing a you—a *you* who is an *I* talking to a *you* who is becoming that *I* while forever slipping back into *you*. You'll see what I mean.

It's also a letter to my self, my younger self, who was always writing letters to his future self. I'm just returning the favor.

To be sure, some names have been changed to protect the innocent. And they are all innocent.

Prologue

Years from now, your lover, who will later be your husband, will read a short story you publish and wonder why you haven't told him about the former boyfriend, the one for whom, in the story, your mother baked cookies. *There was no boyfriend*, you will tell him. But he won't believe you. He will insist that there *must have been* a boyfriend, a secret past, some occluded shadow-story you have either forgotten to share or, worse yet, decided not to divulge. Your lover will believe he has *just cause* to suspect your honesty—not necessarily because you have proven yourself dishonest (though one might argue, as he will upon occasion, that you also haven't fully exonerated yourself from periodic charges of mendacity; after all, omission of the truth, he will remind you, is *a form of lying*). Perhaps, he muses, you are just trying to protect him. Of course you would keep something like this from him, something potentially hurtful. After all, why did your mother extend *to him*—the other, earlier boyfriend—this affectionate gesture, one that she, in his mind, has withheld from him, just as you are now withholding from him the truth about this apparent favorite. Actually, upon further reflection, he suspects you are protecting *her*, shielding your mother from his anger at her having accepted some other boy, having acknowledged some other love of your life, but *not him*. And your protection of her is you valuing her *over* him, which, he might justly say, you've done before and are likely

3

to do again. Hurting him. Undervaluing him. *Loving* him less than he needs or deserves.

There were no cookies, you will maintain. But again, he will not believe you.

In time, you'll understand that inhabiting the space between the real and the imagined has matured into a strategy—not for him, interestingly enough, but for *you*. You will come to realize that, while there were indeed no cookies (you promise!), their presence in the past, written into this story, is nonetheless quite valuable. You took the bare bones of an event—a trip home with some friends, one of whom you were in fact sleeping with (a cute Cajun boy), whom you did in fact introduce to your mother, but not as your lover—and made from it a story of fragile acceptance, of a tentative reaching out, that will become to you far more significant than the things actually seen and experienced. *This is not lying,* you will assert. *It is fiction.*

And some fiction is more accurate than the truth.

1989

"Second Chance"

38 SPECIAL

It's so tempting to begin with the heat of south Louisiana, the wetness of it all, the free-floating mold in the air. You do exaggerate a lot, but it's true when you proclaim, as you always do—or perhaps it's more appropriate to say *you always will*—upon returning to New Orleans or the Gulf Coast, that no place sweats quite like home.

For now, let's start with a scene in summer 1989, you having just graduated with a bachelor's degree in English from Louisiana State University. You are not concerned, like your parents are, about what you will do next. You've already decided. You will be returning to LSU in the fall, with a teaching assistantship, to study comparative literature. This *really* concerns your parents. In fact, it will concern them so much that, shortly before you go off to graduate school—just up the road from where they live and from where you grew up in the greater New Orleans area—you will have a crying and screaming fight with them. But that's a bit later; you don't have to worry about that quite yet.

For now, you are back on I-10 from New Orleans to Baton Rouge, in the backseat of a "parental unit" (what we used to call cars given by parents to their kids), a nondescript but perfectly functioning vehicle that is taking you and four others to a party. Unlike the vehicle, you are not perfectly functioning. You started drinking before you climbed into the parental unit to make the hour-and-a-half-long drive to a student apartment complex neighboring LSU's campus. Right now, you are clutching a fifth of vodka, which you're mixing with orange juice on the spot (shouting that you want your screwdriver "to go!"), but soon you will dispense with the orange juice and just drink straight from the bottle. The others are enjoying the spectacle.

Now we have arrived at the apartment of a person you've never met; you are just tagging along with these folks, only one of whom you know decently. The rest are friends of this friend, and you've only met them a couple of times. You stumble out of the car and into the apartment, already packed with young people drinking and smoking marijuana. It's at this point you stop remembering anything. Oh wait, you will remember sitting down on a couch, then getting up to lurch into the kitchen where your actual friend is making a drink.

Then nothing.

Nothing, that is, until the morning, when you find yourself on the floor of what turns out to be someone's bedroom (same apartment, fortunately), with your friend and his friends yelling from downstairs, "Jonathan, wake the fuck up!" You do, groggy, headachy, dry-mouthed, and roll yourself down to the living room, where your friend tells you that you were "so fucking drunk, man" that you actually scared people. You were yelling and dancing wildly around until you passed out, and a nursing student watched over you for a while. Then your friend and his friends deposited you upstairs to sleep off your intoxication. They considered restraining you, and you wonder why they didn't—sounds like it would've been fun—but you don't voice this opinion.

"Fuck, what else did I do?" you ask, slowly sobering up and beginning to think that you might have *really* embarrassed yourself.

"Well," your friend admits, smiling a little, "you came into the kitchen and felt me up."

That is the last anyone will say of this incident, and you won't entirely believe it, though you won't entirely disbelieve it, either. Later you'll note that you don't see this friend ever again, except for about a week

8

later, when he stops by your house to make sure you're ok. But that's it. That will be it.

This story—not the alleged "feeling up" but the drunkenness, certainly the drunkenness—is not all that unusual for you, though it will seem like one of the more extreme versions of a similar narrative. In fact, at the time you think, *This is one of the more extreme versions of what's been going on, and maybe I should get a fucking grip.*

You will—get a grip, that is—just not in ways you anticipate.

"Straight Up ~ Cold Hearted"

PAULA ABDUL

In your defense, you weren't always like this. I'll even go so far as to say that you were actually *seldom* like you were at that party. You were what people called a "good boy." But then again, perhaps they didn't know you as well as they thought.

You grew up in the Deep South in the '70s and '80s, and no matter what anyone tells you later about that time and place, you know you'd never want to do it over, to experience it again. Not. Ever. You are inclined to hyperbole, for sure, but this one truth you'll hold on to for quite some time. That feeling of *never ever* won't end for you, even as your attitude shifts about south Louisiana, New Orleans, its quirky people and quirky customs, its Mardi Gras, its artery-clogging but still amazingly delicious food, its jazz, its political corruption, its *laissez les bons temps rouler*, its "show me your tits," its completely fucking over-the-top embrace of celebration. Yes, your attitude will slowly change, especially after Katrina, when you'll start to feel somewhat protective of this pocket of the country. But having grown up there, you know that these things are only part of it—part of the hype, part of how the place advertises itself to the rest of the world.

Oh, to be sure, there *is* a Bourbon Street. And later in this story you will find yourself on it, facedown in a puddle of someone else's vomit and piss, pining over a boy. And you will even look back on that episode somewhat fondly; the delights in remembering one's masochistic tendencies made manifest for an audience. *What a time we had*, you'll say. What a time, indeed.

But the "times" do, as you know, *count*; they matter. And the time is 1989. The end of a long reign of error known as the Reagan years, the president whose name will come to adorn so many roads and buildings, including an airport—but a name that would perhaps best be forgotten, one that *will* be forgotten if there's any justice in the universe. Except that you, and many others like you, don't want to forget, not entirely. You can't. And you shouldn't. There's just too much at stake in forgetting atrocities, however much you might want to. There has *always* been too much at stake.

For instance, you remember in 1985—which didn't seem so long ago then, not in 1989—you remember graduating from high school, making the transition to college just a hundred miles up the road, where you thought to yourself, *I will finally feel free. This little faggot will finally be free.* Or so you hoped, desperately: free of all the bullying, all the accusations, all the condemnations, the promises that you—so obviously a femme-boy faggot, a fudgepacker, a queer, a cocksucker—will never be happy, never find love, that you'll only ever find pain and sorrow and regret and violence (fully justified against you) and then a diseased life, a painful death, a lonely death, abandoned, and then the searing fires of hell, the ultimate thing you deserve.

You remember too the boy in high school, one of your classmates, but anonymous, calling on the phone, telling you that your mother should skip buying groceries this week because the next time you go to school you'll be beaten so badly she won't be able to afford the hospital bills. *You little faggot, cocksucking faggot.* You wonder (to this day)—almost marvel—at the specificity of not just the threat but of the aftermath: your mother unable to buy groceries because of the expense of your treatment.

You thought that a hundred miles up the road, in Baton Rouge, you could escape a house, a church, a Catholic school, a community, a city that, despite Mardi Gras and Bourbon Street, really didn't want anything to do with its homegrown faggots. You thought you might be able to start over, be yourself, be something different, be other than what everyone told you you were destined to be. You think, *Is it possible to be anything other than a condemned faggot? Could I be a . . . fabulous faggot?*

In a way, you did become that fabulous faggot. But not as you anticipated, not as you expected. And certainly not in 1985. Or even in 1989.

But wait, some readers are going to want to know: what *about* Mardi Gras and Bourbon Street? Aren't those events and places where the good times do, indeed, roll, where you could've been free, or at least somewhat freer than you were in your suburban life? *Oh no, dear reader. Don't believe the hype.* Sure, some people found temporary solace in the inebriation—cordoned off into a few square blocks a couple of days a year. Some even managed to live their gay lives, and you'll look back on them with admiration and think, *Could I have done the same?* But you didn't, you couldn't. By 1985, the damage had already been done, the lessons learned.

You took them with you, those lessons, wherever you went, with whomever you were connected, with whatever intention or desire you had in your heart. You heard the voices of the kids who taunted you, who called you out, who called you up at home and threatened to take your life; you heard the silences of the teachers and school administrators who brushed it off, saying boys will be boys; you heard the pastor and priest condemn you and your kind to hell; you heard the crying in the night of the few homosexuals depicted in movies or on television; you heard the gasps as Rock Hudson, and then other famous people, revealed that they had AIDS, their bodies wasted, their skulls pushing through their faces; you heard the declarations that AIDS is god's just punishment on the wicked, the forsaken, the already eternally damned.

You remembered the gasps of your own uncle, the only openly gay person you knew, in his hospital bed in 1981, your aunts and uncles surrounding him, watching their brother die. Sure, they must have loved him, somewhat, somehow. But just as surely, they condemned him. He was an object lesson. He was *your* object lesson.

So no, you won't forget—and others like you, growing up in similar places, are not likely to forget—that the president at the time could barely bring himself to mention AIDS. Over and beyond what anyone one else in his party (remember Jesse Helms?) might have thought about faggots, his unwillingness to talk about thousands and thousands of people dying made it abundantly clear that he, and others like him, believed they *deserved* to die.

But you also know that this, while important, is only a part of the story.

"Listen to Your Heart"

ROXETTE

What's easy for you to dismiss when you focus on the damages done—and wow, you *will* focus on those damages, won't you?—is all the other ways, some small, some not so small, you were already preparing for a very different kind of life. You would never forget—because you learned the lesson so well—that any such life, no matter how carefully prepared, was going to be lived in a context not of your choosing. But that was okay. That's what you had to work with. That's what you *have* to work with.

You'll steadily come to see that your existence has been one long, slow, practiced attempt to desire differently, to be other than what you are. *I is an other*, wrote one of your favorite poets—someone you will spend some time writing about in a few years. Right now, in 1989, you are having your own season in hell.

But hell can have its delights, no?

The leader of a country soon to be defunct had announced his intentions to cultivate what he called, in the language of his people, *glasnost* and *perestroika*—openness and restructuring. Little did he know the upheavals that would result, particularly within an economy and political regime that hadn't had much openness and could've used a bit more humane restructuring long ago. But who are we to judge? Where was the openness of your own country's regime?

While you didn't major in political science, you understood—or were at least starting to understand—that the metonymy from the body politic to the body personal suggested any political change you could intuit as good ("Tear down this wall, Mr. Reagan!") might begin with changing your own body, with attention to its wants and desires, with a recognition of how it had been stifled and shaped to conform to others' wishes for it. You couldn't articulate your thoughts, your intuitions, in just those terms, but you felt the increasingly pressing need to experiment, to practice the desires of the body, or at least to pay attention to them.

Inasmuch as you could.

Often, at least at first, you practiced alone. Weekends while you were in college, you'd sometimes go home on the bus, not just so your mother could do your laundry, but also because you could blissfully be alone, as the family often took themselves on Sunday afternoons to Mississippi, to your father's mother's grave. You'd long since decided that you didn't have to make those trips, and your mother, father, and two younger sisters were happy to leave you alone at home, giving them all more space in the car.

You didn't waste time. You stripped down, danced nearly naked around the house. You'd snuck into a showing of *Risky Business* in 1983, when you were still in high school, your first rated-R movie, and you knew, upon seeing Tom Cruise dance around in his tighty-whities, that you had found something you wanted. Your body responded. (To this day, you appreciate a man in white briefs. You wonder why more don't wear them.) So on those Sunday afternoons, home alone, you'd first strip down to your briefs, your slim body, your twink and largely hairless torso, starting to shine with sweat as you rubbed your hands up and down. You'd rub your behind, muscular from years of bike-riding around the city, your initial escapes from home. You were learning to love your behind, but you also wanted to punish it. You picked up the cutting board from the kitchen and bent over a living-room chair and smacked your own ass, hard, and then harder. *Thank you, sir, may I have another?* You didn't have anyone to male bond with, but you imagined your own fraternity of

15

boys who loved paddling ass, who wanted to touch your ass, even if only to inflict a bit of pain on it. Then you'd head to your room, where you'd laid out some otherwise carefully hidden ropes, and you'd practice hog tying yourself, struggling in your bonds. Belts augmented the ropes, and you soon learned that nearly anything, with enough creativity, could be turned into a restraint, an instrument to contain flesh that sometimes felt like it was going to burst open with desire, with need. A sleeping bag? You were on it. Your mother's heating pad for her bad back? You were on it. You stuffed that heating pad into your briefs, belted yourself up, wrapped that sleeping bag around you, rolled over and over to tighten the ropes, all as the heating pad started to toast your bottom. You imagined a punishing scenario in which you, a superhero, were caught and tortured like this, straining to be released so you could save the day. How many times had you seen Adam West and Burt Ward in comparable dire straits, the Joker or Penguin yet again having lured the homosocial duo into some predicament bondage, their bodies turning on a spit and slowly roasting, as though that entire late-'60s television show had just been a surreptitious way to train young boys in masochistic delights? And Batman and Robin were in their briefs too, sported on the outside of their tights, as though showing off their underpants! The heating pad heated up your behind as your thrusts accelerated against your bonds, and before long you were creaming your own tighty-whities, the spasms rocking your body, nearly unbuckling the belts and loosening the ropes that held you in check.

At times, the force of your orgasm would send shockwaves to your toes, which would shudder with delight. You would learn to associate the throbbing of your middle toes with a superior ejaculation, the benchmark you would attempt to achieve again and again—mostly, at first, alone.

"Giving You the Best That I Got"

ANITA BAKER

You wielded that fake paddle on your own ass because no fraternity would
have you, but that wasn't really a problem, was it? You kept to yourself.
You were shy and introverted. You read all the time. Actually, once you
got to college, you dropped the friends you'd made in high school, the
few fellow nerds who would have anything to do with you. You worried
their stench of loserdom would stick to you somehow as you made your
way in Baton Rouge. You are not beyond *being* an asshole, though you ra-
tionalize and justify your behavior in a variety of ways. To be fair, though,
you'd been an outcast for so long, and college was a chance, perhaps
a singular opportunity, to try something different. Not *not* to be a nerd,
but to luxuriate in your nerddom on your own terms.

And also, possibly, just possibly, to be gay.

So no, you didn't *really* want to be in a fraternity, but wow did you
like to follow around the buff boys in their khaki shorts and Greek-
lettered jackets and sweatshirts. This being the Deep South and the
1980s, some of them actually carried around their paddles, and you even
saw a few hazings underway—boys forced to do pushups in the quad,
boys running around in their underwear. How your fantasies were fueled
at nights, in your dorm room, in your stiff bed, your own self stiff under
your mildewy covers, by thoughts of those boys doing sweaty pushups on

each other while big brothers smacked some ass, some brief-clad booty. You jerked off countless times imagining an orgy of boys humiliating and punishing one another until stringy loads of jizz exploded from variously lithe and buff bodies.

No, you didn't need to join the fraternities that wouldn't have you anyway—you, not just too bookish, but also still smacking of the queer. But you also started to not care that you smacked of the queer. Well, perhaps you cared a little. Who wouldn't, especially at that time and in that place? No one you knew was out. No one was even really open. The potential consequences were too dire.

You did, however, make your first forays into self-articulation. You began to tell a few people, usually young women, late at night after a couple of drinks, that you thought about boys, about touching—*you know, touching other young men.* The girls would giggle, hands covering their mouths at the scandalous idea.

One young woman you dated at the time—you'd gone to an all-boys school, and being around young women was kind of exciting, kind of thrilling, so why not date a few, especially if they expressed interest?—this one young woman told you about *her* own homoerotic interests, her thoughts about sleeping with other young women. You laughed and held hands, delighting in the perversity of each other's company.

One night, later, on your nineteenth birthday, she ties you to your bed and whips your ass, over and over. She then flips you over, and you shoot your wad in your tighty-whities while she dry-humps your bony hips. You totally feel like a dirty boy, a bad little dirty boy.

The next day, you both sit outside and read *Great Expectations* for your class in British literature, savoring the long sentences, the illusions and disillusions of Pip, while frat brothers cross the quad in their tight khakis, swatting each other playfully on the butt, oblivious to how you, sitting just a few feet away, are sneaking glances, shifting a bit on your concrete bench to feel the soreness in your own butt from last night's whipping as you think to yourself, *God, I could fuck anything that moves.*

"God, I could fuck anything that moves," you find yourself saying out loud.

Your girlfriend laughs. She knows what you mean. "You only let me dry hump you."

"Yeah, I know."

And then back to *Great Expectations*. Which you most certainly had, but let's face it: you saw Rock Hudson dying of AIDS on national television. Oh, you'd have fun. You *did* have fun. And things are only going to get more intense. But you, and perhaps a whole generation of people just like you—you've read their stories; they are, indeed, out there, that generation of young queer men—you were going to play it safe, not take too many chances.

So for now, you squirm again on that concrete bench, your cock stiffening as you feel the bruised ass cheeks and remember their punishment. At some point, an older version of you will think, *Of course you wanted punishment.* You were raised on a steady diet of homophobia, with AIDS looming as the just judgment for people like you; punishment was the only kind of bodily experience you deserved.

But that's too limited a reading, isn't it? You might have felt you needed to be punished, that that was indeed what you deserved, but you were already pervert enough to turn that punishment into pleasure—and not only pleasure but a *safe* pleasure, one of the safest forms of sexual activity. You were going to make sure—fuck those fuckers—to enjoy your body for as long as you could. You might even say that your generation took seriously the call to explore forms of sexuality that weren't just about raw fucking, cocks probing and invading holes—just what Michel Foucault suggested might happen, with the expansion of the erotic over the whole of the body, beyond the genitals.

Oh, there was still plenty to experience, including the "cocks-probing-holes" thing. But later. We'll get to that soon enough.

"Two Hearts"

PHIL COLLINS

I, for one, do not blame you for dating women, though others, later, will try to persuade you that you were making a mistake, that you were hiding, that you were closeted, that you were even fooling them, being dishonest with them, etc. And most importantly, that you were being dishonest *with yourself.*

But you know that's fucking bullshit. In every conceivable way, you loved the women you were intimate with, such as the one who whipped your ass on your nineteenth birthday. And while in whatever world you might be called "gay" or "queer" or "not straight," it never prevented you from loving these women. Yes, you knew from your late teens on that you wanted to build a life with a man, but you have also built your life with women. One of your oldest friends, perhaps your *closest* friend to this day, is a woman that you have called your nonsexual lifemate—perhaps the only person on the planet who can make your husband jealous because of the bond that you and she have shared for well over two decades.

So, are you bi? For a while, you will call yourself bisexual. That part is coming up. But for now, in 1989, your struggle is to navigate your interest in women along with your drive to engage men sexually. And it's perhaps a bit surprising the extent to which women were not only by your side the entire time but, in some ways, gave you a helping hand.

That's how we arrive at 1989—with you having passed through several relationships, giving heterosexuality the old college try, and pretty much deciding that you needed one year, your final year of college, to see if you could set the record *queer*. Truth be told, there weren't *that* many women, and you were never in danger of inseminating any of them. That was part of the problem. You loved them as friends, you even enjoyed making out with them, and you relished the ones who would whip your ass— but that was about it. Your cock just wasn't otherwise responding.

The ultimate failure here was actually with an older woman, Faith, the church pianist at the little Baptist Christian Indoctrination Center you attended as a teenager.

(Don't forget that you were still going to church at that time. No, of course not, how could you possibly forget? You bear the damages of church-going, of prolonged exposure to Christian indoctrination—damages that fell just short of a priest or pastor sticking his hands down your pants but nonetheless left you questioning yourself—your thoughts, your desires, and the disposition of your eternal soul. But you've told this story before, you've told it many times to others and, more importantly, to yourself. You're committed now to a different narrative.)

Faith, you adored. And she adored you. You freely admit that you enjoyed her company immensely, as well as that of two other older friends— and by older, I mean that you were twenty and they were in their mid-thirties. These "ancients" who attended your church took you under their wing and nurtured your interest in art and music and reading. They were singers and pianists, readers and thinkers. They were open-minded in ways that others in that little Baptist church couldn't fathom. They were your best friends during your junior year in college.

And you fell a little bit in love with Faith. Perhaps she fell a little bit in love with you as well, the two of you sitting side by side at her piano in her tiny apartment, playing duets, you bringing some recent attempts at musical composition. You don't know if she *really* was in love with you, but that Valentine's Day card with the drawn heart and an arrow through it was perhaps a clue.

Perhaps.

You would spend the night at her home, in a separate bed. You would sit next to each other while watching movies, shoulder to shoulder, and you even held her once.

"This isn't so wrong, is it?" She asked you this question, this simple question, as you held her. And of course not; it wasn't wrong at all. But the hug, the holding, wasn't going any further.

She eventually tired of you—or, if not you, of your youth, your inability to commit to something more "adult." Perhaps she had suspicions. You'll never know. But you do know that when she broke off whatever was between you, ramping it down considerably so she could pursue others more open to the kind of love she was looking for, you were heartbroken.

You remain a bit heartbroken about it to this day.

You also know now, as you knew then, that what she did was appropriate, that she needed to move on, that life with you was only ever going to be friendship.

And so as you moved toward the fall of 1988, set to graduate in May of 1989, you wanted to give yourself permission to do something different. You had always wanted to at least *try*. Indeed, you started your freshman year with the hope of doing something different, being a different kind of person. Some good faith efforts were made, some highlights were had.

But now it was time for the full-on approach: queerness in earnest.

"Waiting for a Star to Fall"

BOY MEETS GIRL

Admit it: you had no idea what this would look like. You'd rarely seen any actual out-and-proud queer people. Some readers will find that improbable—but again, the time, the place. Besides your uncle, now dead, who else did you know who was queer? No teachers, though you had your suspicions. Not even in college, where you had still other suspicions and heard rumors. You even once took a poem—remember how embarrassingly bad it was?—to a creative writing professor whom you thought was attractive and whom your girlfriend suggested might be into you.

Here's the scene, just a few years back, a few years before 1989: you and your girlfriend reading flyers tacked up on a bulletin board, looking for opportunities to submit your awful poetry to journals and contests. Some flyer catches your eye. Handsome professor walks up, looks over your shoulder.

"That *does* look interesting."

You chortle, not knowing what to say as the professor walks off.

"Oh my god, he's so into you," whispers your girlfriend.

"What?"

"He was flirting with you!"

"No way."

"Yes way!"

"No."

"You should bring him a poem."

"Hmmm . . . I don't think so."

But you knew you would. And you did. And he thought it was, frankly, terrible, telling you not to spend time rewriting and crafting it, that some work we produce is just to get the crap out of our system. He was most definitely *not* flirting with you then. He never really had been. Your girlfriend was simply trying, if failing, to lend you a hand.

Other women also tried to help out in various ways. Once, under the guise of researching a report on biology and homosexuality, you talked a female friend into accompanying you to a local gay bar. She wasn't fooled, and you know she wasn't. *But what the hell*, she must have thought. *I'll play along.*

You remember the excitement, your pulse pounding, your mouth dry, your attention to the tightness of your jeans, your slicked-back hair. (Ah, the days when you could actually slick back your hair!) A night out at the gay bar with your friend, who also invited along a couple of others.

"This should be good," they all said.

To your collective credit—you, the gay-boy-in-waiting, and your straight friends—you didn't treat this night as a trip to a freak show. No queer circus outing here. Perhaps there's a particular kind of heterosexual privilege you were channeling: the world is yours, and even the gay bars can be part of your expansive playground. But you weren't going, none of you were going, to *make fun* of the gays. Everyone was genuinely curious. You were just curiouser than most.

It wasn't disappointing, was it, that gay bar up Highland Avenue in Baton Rouge? Nieman's, you remember, was its name. The locale would be called different things over the years but largely remain a bar for the queers. Dark, smoky (people could smoke in bars back then), a pounding disco beat with accompanying flashing lights. An empty dance floor. Turns out, you all had arrived too early. You sat, ordered some cocktails, and waited for the crowd to thicken. It did, but perhaps your group was too obviously "straight" looking, because none of you got much play. Except

. . . there was that rather overweight man, perhaps thirty, leaning up against a post, who threw a few smiles your way and started moving in time to the overly loud music. But you turned away, both not attracted to him and also not knowing what you would do even if you were attracted.

After another hour or so, you all started to walk out, past the now-packed dance floor, where you spot a man and woman dancing to the post-disco, pre-techno beats of the 1980s—thumpthumpthumpthumpthump—and a boy catches your eye just as you catch his. He's cute, young, blond, maybe a little pudgy but not unattractively so (you're already vaguely aware of your own internalized fat shaming, now twice in one night, though no one will call it that for quite some time), and then you see him mouth along with the song: "I wanna know what you're thinking. There are some things you can't hide."

You continue on with your friends, not looking back. Just not your time yet.

Not long after, some of the same friends accompany you to a meeting of the lesbian and gay student group, a relatively new thing on campus, something a few of the more venturesome students are trying out. No faculty or staff there. Just a group of twelve, thirteen students sitting in a circle talking about how bad they feel living in a place like Baton Rouge, where gay and lesbian life is so limited, and wouldn't everything be better in a place like, say, New York? Someone starts ranting about how much those kinds of sentiments reek of internalized homophobia, and then a shouting match ensues, and things get *really* ugly when one young queen turns to another young queen and says, "Well, of course you'd think that, being anally receptive."

Talk about internalized homophobia.

You and your friends don't return to these meetings. You pick up a pamphlet, however, that gives precise information about Louisiana's Crime Against Nature law, which, fully in effect at the time if infrequently enforced, criminalizes *any* kind of sexual activity between *any* genders that aren't strictly for reproductive purposes. So, say, a blow job that a wife might give her husband—a crime against nature. Obviously, anything that two (or more) men or two (or more) women might do together—not even *close* to legal.

That was your world, the mid-'80s. So there should be no surprise that it took you a while, even after leaving home, to commit to the year of living queerly. Also worth mentioning: you *weren't exactly rich.* You were the first in your family to go to college, both of your parents being solidly working class—mother, a Cajun from rural Louisiana; father, a hick from Mississippi who pronounced "piano" like "pee-anne-er." She operated a daycare facility; he worked for the power company and drove his truck around town, cutting off lights if people didn't pay their bill. You had scholarships and grants for college (because your parents couldn't afford to send you), but you couldn't exactly say you were "in-dependent"; if you went totally gay and they found out, they might have cut you off, emotionally and financially. You didn't know that they would, but you'd heard that's what happened. It's why your gay uncle had left Cajun country for the big city, escaping the physical abuse of a father who didn't want a faggot as a son. He'd not only been cut off but *beaten out.* You didn't expect a beating, but you didn't expect your gay self to be greeted with open arms.

You knew the risks, and you couldn't always get the image of Rock Hudson, emaciated and caving in on himself, out of your mind. But you still, somehow, perversely, wanted to try. To try to be at least a bit more gay. You had made some interesting first steps, and you were lucky enough to find some friends willing to give you a helping hand (and even a helping swat across your backside). So you decided, in the fall of 1988, you would give yourself the biggest helping hand you could.

"This Time I Know It's for Real"

DONNA SUMMER

You decide to join a club. You'll meet people. You'll be doing something different. You might even find some sympathetic souls with whom you can at least flirt (though you don't have particularly good flirting skills yet). Who knows?

But which club? You haven't ever been much of a team player, not someone who'd participated in sports, not someone who relished the thought of "collective effort," even. More of a loner, a reader, even at times a skulker about. Introverted. But creative. Yes, you're definitely creative. You've enjoyed playing music with others, accompanying singers and flautists and violinists on the piano. So you *do* have some interest in group efforts—but they have to be worthwhile, in your mind, a common cause toward a good purpose, usually aesthetic or intellectual. You are too unattractive—too thin, too cross-eyed, too unkempt with your random hair—to embody a pleasing aesthetic, but you delight in *producing* the aesthetic: jointly making beautiful music, sharing thoughts on books, and art, and movies. . . .

Movies, yes, that's it! There's a film club, a group of undergraduate students, all volunteers, who select most of the films that will be shown in the little movie theater in the Student Union. You could join the Film Committee, as it is usefully called. Perhaps you'll find some other young like-minded homosexuals there. You won't know the possibilities unless you go.

Initially at least, it's what you expect. A bunch of nerdish folk sitting around a table debating what films to bring to campus for students to see. There are limits, of course—a budget as well as oversight committees that make sure the proposals from the Film Committee don't overstep any boundaries, seen and unseen. There are always boundaries, after all.

When you join, the Film Committee is vetting proposals for film series—clusters of movies that explore a topic, an idea, or a filmic gesture. Someone (who will become a friend) proposes, for instance, Voyeurism in Film, a series that will give you a chance to see *Rear Window* on the big screen—or at least a bigger screen than the television at your parents' home. Fun stuff like that. Intellectual, even.

You have an idea for a film series, but you're not putting it out there, not quite yet.

First, you want to make friends. The chair of the committee (the one who will become a friend) is actually someone you had a class with— honors biology—and with whom you participated on a group project, Biology in Shakespeare, the kind of thing Humanities majors do in honors biology classes. That was a couple of years ago, but there's at least a history there, a place to start. And she's cute, and very smart.

You propose a coffee or drink, and she eagerly accepts. Cool. You're off to a good start! It's not long before you and she and some of the other folks on the committee are regularly going out and drinking at the local collegiate pub, or the dive bar on State Street, or a place called The Library (so students could legitimately say, when asked by inquisitive elders, that they were "at the library"), and then winding up in various dorm rooms.

In time your little group would consist of you, K, C (who also worked on the school's newspaper staff as a cartoonist), L, and R (L's boyfriend). You won't later remember what any of these people majored in, but they were all a bit artsy, read a lot, and drank a lot. That sufficed for you, especially post-Faith and as your older church friends took a backseat to your new friends, your new commitment to living large in your senior year. Living large, living *queer*.

You, of course, were majoring in English, much to your parents' chagrin. They actually weren't too horrified by it (they'll be more concerned about your decision to go on to graduate school) because they weren't paying for it. You survived on grants and scholarships, babysitting for friends of your parents, and working as an English tutor for pocket money, which really meant, during your senior year, drinking money. You made good grades and, as an honors student, had just started writing your senior thesis. You chose Professor Collins to direct it, having taken his class on British Farce, where you first read novels by Ronald Firbank and plays by Joe Orton, as well as work by Oscar Wilde and Evelyn Waugh. Of the four, only Waugh wasn't an avowed homosexual, but, hey, c'mon, you'd devoured *Brideshead Revisited* in high school, seen the television miniseries with Jeremy Irons, Anthony Andrews, Sir John Gielgud, and Sir Laurence Olivier. Gay, gay, gay, so very gay, even for a novel by a Catholic writer about Catholic aristocrats coping with severe family dysfunction, including the homosexuality of one of its handsome but alcoholic fair-haired sons, Sebastian Flyte. You focused your attention on the first half of the book and the first half of the tv series, in which Charles and Sebastian basically fall in love while attending Oxford, a charming late-adolescent romance—the kind you wished you'd had but didn't—and you will forever remember the scene in which Sebastian's younger sister surprises the two friends while they are sunbathing in the nude. Such pale but cute asscheeks. And on television! Piped into your parents' home! What luck, what sheer fucking luck! (Though you were glad no one saw you watching this.)

So yes, English, your chosen field of study. It was the compromise major since music seemed too difficult a financial road to travel, no matter how much you loved playing the piano, listening to music, even composing little pieces (and trying your hand at some bigger pieces too; molding in a box in a future closet will be the sketches of orchestral scores, pencil marks fading with time). Your parents believe that, with

English degree in hand, you will be able to come home, get a job teaching at the local high school, buy a house down the street, marry a sweet girl, and settle down into the rest of your life.

As Ronald Firbank might write, ". . ."

". . .," you think.

That's the plan, *their* plan. So of course you are going to do everything you can this final year, your senior year, to try something new, see if there *is* a way to live differently. Or at least to experiment with some other kind of life before you are fixed in this picture of professional and domestic "bliss."

(You are desperate. You wouldn't characterize it that way, but you are.)

That's perhaps why, a couple of meetings into your participation on the Film Committee, you start to fall in love with Matt. *Oh, Matt. Beautiful Matt.* To this day, *something about Matt.* A bit chunky, though not fat. Definitely not a twink, though. Piercing pale-blue eyes. A swoop of brown hair over his forehead, drifting at times over one eye. He knows this is attractive. He might stand in front of the mirror in the mornings and play with that little lick of hair, twisting and turning it down so it will fall just so. And so smart, obviously so smart. A bit snarky. Not a snippy queen. Not a queen at all, apparently. A dude, a regular dude, but also one not afraid of his own intelligence. A columnist for the student newspaper. Someone with *ideas*, with thoughts, even provocative thoughts. You realize that you start going to the meetings just to be near him, to be in his presence, to hear what he has to say, just to enjoy the contrarian thoughts he sends into the room. He's argumentative. He's bold and confident, characteristics that, even more than his smooth and pale plump cheeks (face *and* ass), you come to admire.

So begins the slippage between "I want to be like you" and "I want you." A fine line, that. You cross it. You definitely cross it. But Matt hasn't a clue. One day, heading from class back to your dorm, a sad room with no air-conditioning in a hundred-year-old former army barracks, you see him walking toward the campus quad. He passes right by. How many weeks have you both been on the committee together? He doesn't know you, or if he does, he doesn't acknowledge you. You're not worth his notice yet. *Yet*, you think; *we might be able to change this.* And then you realize something *really* exciting: he's clearly walking *from your own dorm. He must live in Pentagon! Oh my fucking god! You're neighbors!*

"I'll Be Loving You (Forever)"
or "Cherish"

NEW KIDS ON THE BLOCK / MADONNA

At first, you confine yourself, and content yourself, with the unfortunately infrequent Film Committee meetings, where you can at least be in his presence. Then, to your delight, while you're out with your little crew—K, C, L, and R—you run into Matt and a few other people, *his* friends from the committee, people whose names you will not long remember but whose faces you can conjure if you try: some obnoxious female undergrad; a balding graduate student, male; and another graduate student, bespectacled, brown hair, but as obnoxious as the others. What Matt sees in these people, you have no idea.

Such encounters, as your different crews collide at the local pub, the dive bar on State Street, or wherever, are never satisfying. The banter is thick amongst the separate groups, but the exchanges between them otherwise limited, with little cross-fertilization. His crew pays you no mind. More importantly, *he* pays you no mind.

Whatever, you think. You have your pride, after all.

But other plans hatch when you discover that your roommate, Nick, a Taiwanese student studying abroad for the year, plays soccer with Matt at least weekly. They aren't really friends but share the camaraderie of sport. *Soccer.* The little silky shorts. The pumping legs sticking out of those little silky shorts. You immediately wish you knew a helluva lot more about soccer.

You're not at all interested in your roommate, so how do you know that he and Matt play together? Well, sitting in your dorm room late one afternoon, reading or jerking off, you hear voices outside: Nick's accented English accompanied by someone else's voice, a voice you've heard before, a voice that all but calls you to lean into it, to pay more attention, a voice deep but as silky as the soccer shorts you spy as you peep through the blinds to confirm, yes, yes, indeed: Matt!

It takes only a little convincing to talk Nick into inviting him—and you—out for a drink. After all, the three of you know each other, sort of. Will this delicate triangle be sturdy enough to support sharper angles? What geometric possibilities await? (Such are the analogies that appeal to you at the time.)

The answers, alas, are no and none. The couple of times you all get together, once at least at that dive bar on State Street, consist of the two of them talking sports while you wilt in a chair, your screwdriver's ice cubes steadily diluting both your drink and your dreams of taking a slightly drunken Matt back to your, or better yet his (no Nick!), dorm room. Your attempts at humor fall flat; your desire to bond over film remains unfulfilled; your feigned interest in journalism he snuffs out as the deception it is.

You sit in your chair in the dive bar, sipping watered-down vodka, and your desire turns a darker shade, becomes the desire for vengeance. After all, if this pale and pudgy little twat won't have you, perhaps he needs to be punished?

Your first round of attack is on his turf: the student newspaper. Matt has just written a column, supposedly extolling the virtues of free speech, arguing that the "classic" pornographic film *Deep Throat* should be screened at the Student Union. You don't recall him advocating for this in committee; perhaps you missed it; perhaps you didn't care because, at

33

the time, you were less taken with the content of his speech and focused instead on the glory of him speaking at all. But now your eyes are open; the scales have fallen. *He's a pig.* You write your own editorial, countering Matt, rebutting his stupidity in arguing for such an exploitative piece of trash. You don your best Matthew Arnold, proclaiming that only the best that has been known and thought should be allowed in the hallowed halls of our precious Student Union, one of the last truly free spaces for open deliberation and the exchange of ideas, a forum worthy of the ancients. Why sully it with porn? With *filth*?

Back at your dorm, while Nick is out playing soccer, you strip to your briefs and hump your thin mattress, imagining Matt tied to the bed, the same bed that your girlfriend had once tied you to, but this time *you* are in control, your victim facedown, naked and gagged. You take a cucumber and slowly start to sodomize him. *Reject me, you pudgy motherfucker? I'll teach you a thing or two.* And you jizz your tighty-whities while the Matt in your mind squirms, frightened, and moans and begs for release.

What a sick and twisted fuck you are.

The newspaper prints your editorial, though you can't verify anyone has read it. (You'll keep a copy, buried in a box, for years and years; it may very well still be in some crate in your garage. But that's all in the future, the far, far future.) More to the point, the transformation that you expected from your counter-column—a contrite Matt calling you up, inviting you to grab a beer to express how you've opened his own eyes, or even just to air your differences and agree to disagree . . . some opportunity for the two of you, just the two of you, without Nick, to talk—none of that happens. Matt is as cool and distant as ever.

So, next strike. You're not done yet. This one you bring closer to home.

It's about time for the Film Committee to select its next thematic series, and you propose—in the fall of 1988—Homosexuality in Film. That's right. You say it. You put that shit right out there. You are coming out. Publicly. Sort of. Well, at least on the Film Committee. And only by implication. If you can't have Matt through little tricks and arranged meetings, then perhaps you can attract—or at least wow—him by your boldness, your audacity, your sheer avant-garde pluckiness.

We'll see how that goes in a bit. But first . . .

"Love Shack" or
"Sowing the Seeds of Love"

THE B-52S / TEARS FOR FEARS

You have already, basically, started to "come out" to your friends, the little crew of K, C, L, and R. It is a fragile crew, and you know this—each of you, for your own reasons, banding together, experimenting, exploring. Having fun, yes, but everything feels a bit thrown together, messy, driven by drink and hormones. While L and R are girlfriend/boyfriend, L is soon sleeping with C as girlfriend/girlfriend, and while you are invested in pursuing your queer desires, you also regularly make out with C, the cartoonist for the school paper. Do you think that making out with C will get you closer to Matt, her proximity via the newspaper a way to feel his vibe, however attenuated?

But there is something always, uh, *between* you and C, some interference. You lie in bed with her, your dorm bed, in your dorm room, which actually appears in some of her cartoons about the follies and foibles of campus life. You're making out. She wants to go further. You take her hand and put it on your crotch.

"I like you. I really do. You're a great friend, a really, really cool friend, but see? I'm just not oriented that way."

"Who cares?"

36

And so the kissing continues, the necking, a hickey or two that your mother will spy when you next go home and decide not to comment upon.

Another way to express it is that there is ultimately *nothing* between you and C, or more precisely, an emptiness that you want to inhabit with someone else. (That emptiness will remain, and years later, when you befriend each other on Facebook, it will evince itself through the lack of messages, the paucity of comments and likes, the inability to find anything, really, to talk about—though surely there must be something, you'll think. There must be *something*.) But part of the purpose of the crew is to fill up the time, the anxious time, the age of anxiety before the shit really hits the fan, when things will get real, when decisions will have to be made. The deadline looms. This last year feels so spacious, until it doesn't.

No matter how you view it, you will not leave this year the same. You will think of one of your favorite poets, writing to his teacher as he embarks on his own adventures of somatic and aesthetic debauchery: "I is an other." And for you, much as it was for that poet, substances and sex play a role in the aesthetics and somatics of transformation.

A typical afternoon sees you all meeting in a dorm room, usually yours, given its location between a dining hall and the student ghetto surrounding State Street. You gather, debrief about the day, and then head to happy hour, which seems a discovery, an amazing find, as you can drink cheaply. And you do. Your favorite cocktail quickly becomes something called Jet Fuel, which looks like Windex in a shot glass. You only really need one, but sometimes you have two. What the hell? You're young. You're confident your liver will recover. (Truth be told: you never once give a thought to your liver.)

When happy hour comes to an end at any one of the bars that the crew haunts, it's time to stumble back toward campus—and you're all often stumbling—to hit the dining hall before it closes. From the outside, your group doesn't seem that rowdy. You are all, after all, honors students; you know that you shouldn't *look* drunk in public, much less on campus, even if this *is* Louisiana, home of the City That Care Forgot. Sometimes, though, it's a bit obvious that you and yours have had a little to drink, and the cafeteria ladies smile and wink. There are some tender moments, one you'll never forget: C, somewhat disoriented, a cafeteria lady taking her tray from her and leading her to a table.

You get through dinner and head back to a dorm room—again, usually yours, the one that appears in C's cartoons. (Once, as you sit in a class, you open the student paper and recognize the scene, only a bra appears draped over the lamp sitting on a milk crate by your bed, and you audibly gasp in a way that startles the people around you.) You all lounge around on your bed, dog-piling, still drunk but now heavy with food. Some of you make out. Some of you fall asleep. Some of you fall asleep while making out. Some of you stay, some stumble back to their own dorm rooms. It's only ten or so at night. You started early, after all—the joy of happy hour—and by nine the next morning, you're all wide awake and ready for class, no harm done, enough sleep accomplished to refresh your young bodies, resilient and ready for more.

You feel smart. You all feel so smart, so clever, the creams of your various crops. You're improving the art of drinking to excess. You've got this. You've got this down. You pretentiously call yourselves the New Decadence.

Even the decadence can't escape the fact that you're all living in Louisiana, in the Deep South, with most of your parents practicing some version of totalitarian Christianity. Consequently, the New Decadence is a bit more studied, more practiced, with periodic bouts of moderation. Every once in a while, the crew decides to take a break. *Maybe tonight we don't drink. It's Tuesday, after all.* Though you agree that drinking on Wednesdays and Thursdays is the best—something so deliciously transgressive about getting fucked up in the middle of the week—you do need a hiatus at times. You want to be able to keep this up. So you all go to the movies. (You *are* on the Film Committee.) Or you attend a lecture, something to demonstrate to yourselves that you're engaged in intellectual life at a research university.

L and R are still boyfriend/girlfriend, even as L sleeps with C. But whatever. People experiment. Then you and C decide that you too should experiment, that you should have what you call "heterosexual night out." You're both committed to exploring your homosexual selves, but that's not always possible—Matt still ignores you, and L has to spend *some* nights with R—so you two go out for a night, which is frankly more of the same: happy hour, cafeteria, making out on your bed, though you and she don't make out *that much* because you both know what you really want.

One such night out, you and C go to a lecture instead, a lecture being held in the same theater space where the committee's films are shown. It's an exceedingly strange lecture in which a professor of art argues that the brushstrokes of various modernist artworks actually encode in the strokes themselves the phallic and Oedipal desires that are at the heart of psychosexual development—at least from the Freudian perspective. Think Kandinsky, swirls and lines, the raw and unsymbolic expression of libidinal thrusts and resistances.

You find it completely exhilarating.

C and you leave the auditorium, head to the bar, the one with Jet Fuel, discussing the merits and demerits of the lecture, including the professor's rather staid dress for such a scandalous topic, but you are nonetheless on fire with the possibility that the sexual—that *sex*—might saturate *everything,* that art isn't symbolic of sex, that art *is* sex, the strokes of a painter's brush the dynamic thrusting and pulsing of the erotic itself. You start to talk about the choral finale of Beethoven's ninth symphony, the "Ode to Joy," the German poet Schiller's paean to brotherhood, to political fraternity across the globe. Over first one and then another cocktail, you're enough of a nerd to be talking with C about this symphony, this poem, the climactic moments (and climactic isn't a pun here, you realize) when the chorus, already ecstatic in their exaltation of the unity of mankind, the joy of fraternity—"Deine Zauber benden wieder, Was die Mode streng geteilt"—erupts with an ejaculatory command—"Seid umschlungen! Seid umschlungen!": "Be embraced! Be embraced!" you millions, you countless hordes, you unwashed masses. (Oh wait, different poem.) You can't help but hear in this command—punctuated as it is in the chorus, accented heavily (BE embraced, BE embraced)—no, you can't help but hear in this phrase something a bit TOO forceful, a nonconsensual hug, something creepy approaching, a transgression. You all *will* be joyful with our fraternity, which reaches out to wrap its arms around you, to smother you with its love.

Even here, you proclaim, even in this ode to joy, this classic hymn from the heights—and depths!—of the Enlightenment, yes, even here, sex, sex, sex everywhere, everywhere the libidinal thrust, the Id, the shockingly vital currents of desire, pulsing, coursing, throbbing . . .

What a good year this is turning out to be. At least you're *talking* a lot about sex.

"Stand" or "What I Am"

BAND / EDIE BRICKELL

No wonder you feel particularly alive the next week when you go into the Film Committee meeting with typed copies of your proposal. It's one page. That's all you need. *What could be more current? What could be more pressing?* you argue. AIDS has made homosexuality a topic of international conversation, if not outright consternation, and increasingly the film industry has been responding with more portrayals of gays and lesbians. Hell, even before AIDS, in the aftermath of the Stonewall riots, there'd been a steady increase of homos in the movies, as Vito Russo demonstrates in *The Celluloid Closet*—a book that traces representations of queers in film from long *before* Stonewall. Yes, your time has come. You're barely out of the closet, and you haven't even had any homo sex yet, but you know what you want—Homosexuality in Film.

What films do you propose? Top of the list: *Making Love*, a film that you will blush to see later in life, it's so bad. But hey, there's also *Cruising*, with Al Pacino! Certainly, it had a rocky start, with gays protesting the portrayal of a serial killer in the queer BDSM underground of New York. Maybe not the most flattering way to present homos to the skittish straights, but fucking hot nonetheless! And then *Parting Glances* and *Desert Hearts*—oh my god, two film *classics* from recent years. You remember sneaking to the movie theater off campus to see them both just a couple of years earlier, and then taking one of your girlfriends—the one who was curious about lesbian sex—to see *Desert Hearts*. *Ooh la la*. She was so turned on. She practically attacked you later that night.

In your excitement, you're not prepared for the tepid response that greets your proposal. Sure, C and L and R support you, but not many others. And, salt in the wound of his tacit rejection, Matt—*MATT!*—leads the charge *against* your proposal, he and his friends questioning the worth of the films on your list. *Making Love? Really?* In retrospect, you see their point. But, but . . . in the moment, in the moment of your own liberating steps out of the closet, you feel this questioning as the double rejection it is: not only does Matt not want to pay you any attention, but when push comes to shove, when you've extended yourself in this bold and brave way, he's willing to say, "Nope. Let's not do this. What about Animation in Film?"

What the fuck? They want *children's* films as opposed to *sex*!? Indeed, they do. And so do most of the other members of the Film Committee, who vote against your proposal in favor of cartoons.

"Miss You Like Crazy"

NATALIE COLE

That night, in the bar, over your shot of Windex, you and C and L and R commiserate. So much unfairness. Just so much. You have a hard time shaping your anger and outrage, tinged with bitterness and sadness, into anything remotely resembling a political position. That will come in time. For now, though, this feels like just another rejection. A boy who won't love you, his cool disdain registering in your mind and in your gut as the hostility of exclusion, the kind of exclusion you'd felt for so long, growing up and attending Catholic school, going to church, learning about how the homosexuals are the wretched of the earth, outcast and unclean: *You are not one of us. You are not part of the tribe. We don't want your kind here.*

This is one of the reasons you drink. Well, it *does* taste good, that glass of Windex. For a shot, it goes down very smoothly. And, as you know, you only need one, maybe two on a tough night, but *the numbness, the loving numbness—can there be a more beautiful sensation in the world?* The fact that you turn to C and ask her this question suggests you haven't lived enough yet.

Indeed, you haven't. What you desire, what your body turns toward in the middle of the night, rolling over your erection, both hiding it in the small hours of the dark and rubbing it against your sweaty sheets—what that dick wants, you suspect it might never get. Or not get easily at all.

Not that you haven't tried. Even in high school, you reached out in your fumbling way. D, the Latino boy who populated your fantasies, was so gorgeous in his black pea coat, a striped button-down with a bit of hot pink t-shirt sticking out at the collar. *So fucking hot.* And perhaps that t-shirt was sending a signal, some sign of openness, of a willingness to experiment. In fact, he *was* "open," he and his friends—some of the smarter but also snarkier kids in your class.

But no, D, even with his hot pink t-shirt, wasn't as open as you hoped, and your attempts to lure him to your house, ostensibly to listen to music and to talk but really just to be close enough to smell him, were limited and unsatisfactory. He was likely wise to you—or maybe not? Perhaps he just didn't feel you, jibe with you, wasn't on the same wavelength, even as friends. He was, after all, so cool, so very fucking cool. And you? Well . . . not.

But a crush can be a long-lived thing, and your heart skips a beat when you see him on campus, when you turn a corner and there he is, greeting you with his big smile as he rushes past. You had no idea he had enrolled at LSU. You tell your girlfriend, later that night, that you ran into the boy you had a crush on in high school. She laughs. She likely whips your ass extra hard the next time she gets a chance. You wonder at times if that isn't your primary sexual orientation—ass-whipping. It's a very particular kind of orientation, when you stop to think about it. You've enjoyed having your ass whipped by young women, and you can definitely imagine spanking the crap out of some young man, but you don't want to strike a woman's behind. Honestly, you don't want anything to do with a woman's ass. This is all about the male butt—his or yours. It will often, for you, now and for quite some time, be all about the male butt, yours or someone else's.

Your girlfriend thinks of her own lesbian interests. Your relationship is a resonance chamber of misdirected desires—but then again, what desire is ever so directly pointed that it follows a true and narrow path? Let's not entertain too broadly universalizing thoughts on the ontological trajectory of desire. Suffice it to say that, in this time and place, with the particular constraints of your southern Louisiana working-class background at the ascent of the AIDS epidemic, nationally televised for others' entertainment and your edification—suffice it to say that your somatic and psychic being is doing the best it can to function, to keep you alive, to keep you from a descent into neurotic or even psychotic tics and states. A little misdirection is to be expected.

And so, too, a little pursuit of numbness.

"Another Jet Fuel, please?"

As you sink into slumber later that night, after the rejection by the majority of the Film Committee, something in you realizes, though you can't articulate it, that you can't let this rejection stand. Not this time. Something is going to happen. You don't know what yet. But something. And then the swirls of dream take over and you sink, one hand cupping an ass cheek, into alcohol-induced visions of what to you has always been, up to now, the almost inexpressible.

"Eternal Flame"

THE BANGLES

Because you are an honors student, part of this final year is taken up with researching and writing a thesis—in your particular case, a fifty-page analysis of the poetry of Wilfred Owen and Georg Trakl, who wrote and died during World War I.

You've always adored poetry. You always will. Poetry was your first literary love. Even before you became a fantasy and science fiction nerd, you'd memorize and recite poems for extra credit in fifth-grade language arts class because your scores were otherwise mediocre. You didn't love books then, not really. Assigned texts, like *The Prince and the Pauper*, went unread, and you only intermittently paid attention to the broadcast of the old movie based on it. To be fair, you did enjoy parts of *Little Men*. The girls had been assigned *Little Women*, and too bad for them, because *Little Men* had some juicy bits. The novel is set in the unconventional school run by Professor Friedrich and Mrs. Josephine Bhaer (what Jo March grows up to do with her older husband), where a cast of miscreant boys get into various scrapes and troubles, acting out their anxieties and exploring different vices. In one scene, a particularly bad boy seems like he's about to get thrashed by the professor, but in a surprise turn, the professor hands him the cane and bends over, telling the boy to punish him for failing to teach the young man to behave better.

The poor kid makes a feeble strike or two and then bursts into sobs, embracing the older man, whom he doesn't really want to hurt. What young pervert wouldn't thrill to this scene. You even cajoled your friends, all on the cusp of puberty, to act out this proto-sadomasochistic spectacle of intergenerational power exchange. There's another section in which a young girl (yes, there are apparently some girls associated with this school) is taught a lesson about her proper place by having a rope tied around her waist for the afternoon, the other end attached to a chair or some other object that fixes her on a leash. *Ooh la la*. You all playɛd out that interlude as well, alternating between bondage and spanking.

Years later, in 1988, 1989, sitting at the little card table you use as a desk in your dorm room, you have advanced to scenes of global bondage and punishment, delighting in the pathos of the war poets, their verses saturated with the tragedy of men sent to the front lines, youth cut off in its prime, possibility and potential eliminated before it even had a chance to flower. Take Wilfred Owen's "Arms and the Boy," for instance:

Let the boy try along this bayonet-blade
How cold steel is, and keen with hunger of blood;
Blue with all malice, like a madman's flash;
And thinly drawn with famishing for flesh.

Oh boy, the blade, hungry for blood and famishing for flesh! Of course, you thrill to this language, whose Freudian undertones are practically screaming at you, Owen himself wanting to feast on the flesh of the young men in his unit. But there's also plausible deniability here, a weird kind of closeting that one can sneak into if necessary. No one looking at the verse could deny your assertion that this is about war, about young men sacrificed to the machinations of political powers (which made little sense at the time and makes even less with the passing years), but *you* know there's more to it. And even at your thesis defense, when asked what you would do had you more time, where you would take the project next, you say that you would want to explore issues of sexuality—Owen's homoeroticism but also Trakl's possible incestuous desires. Yes, something about the sexual calls to you, and you can identify it, even if you don't write about it explicitly in your thesis.

This verse resonates with you in other ways, too, though you can't quite articulate the twistier, darker contours of that identification. Like the boys the poet writes about, you see yourself, deep inside, as *wasted youth*, cutoff potential, cut down *before your prime*. You don't really think you'll survive. You give yourself to thirty. That's it. That's how unimaginable living a queer life is for you. That's how damaged your sense of possibility is.

Yes, you can experiment now. And you do. You *are* experimenting. But it's more like pretending. You go home some weekends so mother can do your laundry, and she doesn't comment on the semen stains in your underwear, the signs that you've violently jerked off into your tighty-whities. She doesn't want to know what you're imagining. No one there does. And while at home, you sometimes don't want to know it yourself. You stop by church, where, of course, your desires are not welcome. You see your (formerly so close) older friends. You see the nightly reports about the spread of AIDS, the protests, the government "action" having moved from condemnation of queers, through silence on the topic, to talk about sending the infected to "camps." And then you think of your uncle, who was gay, who died years ago, his life still an object lesson.

Back at school, every now and then you see on campus a tall Black queen, a young man with a bit of a swish, a lisp, someone who can't quite hide and realized long ago that it would take too much energy to pretend anyway. And since he's Black in the Deep South to boot, it's not as though hiding his queerness is going to drastically improve his situation. *So, what the fuck*, you imagine him saying. *What the fuck, really. Why not just be who I am, want what I want, and the consequences be damned?* But all of this is projection, imagining what someone else might be capable of doing—making the turn from potential despair to possible defiance—and imagining in someone else's life what you so often have such a hard time imagining for yourself.

"Baby, I Love Your Way"

WILL TO POWER

And then you meet Mike. You won't remember the exact sequence of events, but Mike (you know even as you meet him) is a turning point. You first encounter him—and you do remember it, you *will* remember it—hanging out in the Film Committee cubicle in the maze of offices in the Student Union, both of you looking through film catalogs. This is before you formally propose your series Homosexuality in Film, and Mike likely sees you lingering over the gay-themed content. His interest is, perhaps, piqued. He engages you in conversation. You discuss your majors. You talk about your thesis. *Oh, you study German?* You do, you do. *I'm taking German right now. Oh, those verbs* . . . You know, you know.

When you part, heading for separate classes, you think, *Cute, cute.* And he *is* most definitely cute. You're not going to lie to yourself: he's not *devastatingly* attractive. He's not Matt. He's tall and thin, with short red hair tending to curl, a bit bookish looking even with his stylishly heavy-framed glasses, maybe even a trifle awkward. But obviously not totally straight if also obviously not totally gay—a combination you come to recognize in others, perhaps even in yourself, the combination that can't pull off full-frontal heterosexuality but also doesn't want to be too flamboyant. This could be attractive to you, you think. (You also think with shame about the young Black queen, the one who likely *cannot*

49

pass, who never stood a chance, and you wonder, even now, is your shame about your pity for him, about wanting to protect him, or are you ashamed for thinking, *Thank god that's not me?* So much to ponder here. Always so much.)

Anyway, you don't dwell *too much* on Mike, because there's Matt, *too much* Matt. But you don't forget about him, either. Later Mike admits he was tempted to stop by your dorm room, slip a note under your door, ask you for help with those troublesome German verbs, and you'll wonder if you felt the vibe, if you were attuned somehow to Mike's interest, at least his curiosity. That interest, that curiosity . . . it is your biggest aphrodisiac, even as it's not necessarily the thing you fall for. You fall, all too often, for the unobtainable. More on this later, for sure, but suffice it to say for now that Matt's cool disdain slays you while Mike's curiosity intrigues you—and sometimes, when you can't slay back, a little intrigue is all you need.

One night, after your proposal has been shot down in the Film Committee—*Matt! O Matt! The betrayal!*—you find yourself getting trashed with K and L (now an item) and likely R (still hanging on to L) and C (who knows you're good for a make-out session if little else), and somehow your crew also meets up with Mike. Perhaps he's out on the town. Perhaps he's been following you. Perhaps he's become aware of your midweek drinking habits. You don't know, but you're really glad to see him—delighted, in fact, given the horrors of the recent rejections—and so you all sit in the pubbish bar and get drunk. You then stumble back to your dorm room, and everyone collapses on the two beds, your own and the one that's now vacant because you asked Nick to move out. You wanted your own room, because even then you had a feeling that things were going to get interesting, that the fun was about to begin, that the experimentation of your little crew was about to launch in earnest. And it does. K and L are making out on one bed, and you're sitting with Mike on the other, and in your inebriated state you stretch out on the mattress, tired but not unpleasantly so, and then Mike is stretching out next to you, curling into you, moving his body on top of yours, and then you feel his face getting closer to your own, closer and closer, and then his lips are on yours and the first thing, the very first thing you notice about your very first kiss from a man, a kiss full on the lips, is that he has stubble.

He has stubble.

And it's rough. It's startling. But it's not wrong. It's right, totally right, those little hairs you hadn't noticed, circling his mouth, pricking you— and you wonder, *Can he feel my stubble? Is this a surprise to him too?* You immediately grow suspect of such thinking, though, like you're trying to get out of this moment, this moment finally happening, so you dive back into his lips, opening your mouth, opening his mouth, and you are happy, you are happy, and someone in the room, maybe L, maybe K, says, "I'm so happy for Jonathan." And you are happy that she is happy, whoever is happy for you, because you need what you are doing in this moment to be shared—not just with Mike, who is most definitely sharing it with you, his tongue sharing your tongue—but with someone else, someone witnessing this, someone who is *happy for you*. You've never had this kind of recognition before. You've never felt *this seen*.

"If I Could Turn Back Time"

CHER

It doesn't last long.

I should've offered, I suppose, what you will later know as a "spoiler alert," but even you, in 1989, didn't imagine it could go on as long as it does, which is a month, a bit over a month. Not that you and Mike don't have some fun. You really do. But it's mostly more of the same—getting together with the group, drinking, drinking, drinking, stumbling back to a dorm room, usually yours, fumbling with clothes, making out, passing out. It's a good routine, you think, for the boring weekday nights. Some weekends, you skip the trip home and repeat the routine on a more traditional Friday or Saturday night.

All that drinking isn't necessarily good for your sexual performance, even if it lowers your inhibitions. Mostly you just suck each other off, but you can tell, you can already tell, that Mike wants more. You foolishly ask him once, while he's sucking you off, what he wants, what he *really* wants, and he immediately slides his finger up your ass. But you're not ready for that. You don't mind having your ass slapped, or even slapping a boy's ass (and Mike's got a great little trim behind), but you don't want *that* up there, not yet, maybe not ever, seeing as how you've been traumatized by AIDS, which you're glad is already in ALL CAPS because you'd have to write it in ALL CAPS—AIDS—even if it weren't.

It's still fun, even as Mike grows bored with your sexual inexperience. Before that happens, though, other stuff will make your life all the more interesting. And not in a good way.

Let's start with the weekend of St. Patrick's Day. You stay up at LSU on Saturday, but you've arranged with the crew to drive to your parents' home on Sunday so you can all attend the holiday parade your mother is so fond of. Before that, you have two weekend nights in which to drink, party, carouse, etc.—as usual.

Friday, however, Mike has other plans—which sounds mysterious to you, and is perhaps a warning, a sign, a *warning sign*—but you don't worry about it and head out for your regular happy hour followed by dining hall followed by collapsing into drunken slumber. But it turns out this isn't a usual Friday night. You are *particularly* intoxicated. Perhaps you fret over where Mike is, what he's doing, why he has "other plans," why you aren't included in them? Then again, your relationship is pretty casual. You only meet up once or twice a week. You're not exactly glued at the hip, though you like his hips, trim as they are, the curve into his crotch. But you've only really had a handful of dates, including a lovely evening out to see *Torch Song Trilogy*, the Harvey Fierstein play that he adapted for the big screen, with Fierstein himself in the main role and Matthew Broderick—young and delicious Matthew!—as the love of his life who is (spoiler alert!) tragically killed. Despite this sad ending, the film nonetheless gives you some powerful lines, some potent ways to talk about your emerging life. In the aftermath of his lover's death, Harvey's character is confronted by his former lover, a really closeted man, who would like to resume their relationship. But Harvey, having just ousted his own mother from his house for not accepting him, throws down the terms, the only terms, on which he is willing to live: "Ed, Angel, I just threw my mother, my mother! Out of the house, all she wanted was to not talk about it. Do you really think I'm gonna ask less from you?" Stunning. Even you, *even you as you are in 1989*, know that these lines will stick with you the rest of your life. You won't know at the time how to live up to them. But you will find out. For now, though, they mark a turning point—even if you can't imagine not being in the closet, or throwing your mother out of your house, or demanding respect from those who would be your lovers.

You aren't there yet. You are, instead, much more than usually drunk on this Friday night, without your lover, with your friends, and you get angry, unaccountably angry (but, of course, there *is* an accounting for it, this anger). Back at your dorm room, continuing to drink, this time a cheap gin that you all pass around, you begin to rant and rave about the unfairness of things, so much unfairness, those fucking bastards, those gay-haters, those guys who voted down your proposal.

And Matthew, MATT! How could he? He could lobby for Deep Throat—*DEEP FUCKING THROAT!—but not for Homosexuality in Film? What the fuck!?*

You lurch out of your room, your friends in tow, some of them half-heartedly trying to restrain you. Crossing the quad between your building and Matt's, you continue to shout, *Those fuckers, those fuckers, it's time to confront those fuckers*. You take another swig from your bottle and are frankly unsure how you make it up to his floor, stumbling all the way, C and K laughing and pawing at you, and you start banging on his door. But he's not home. *The fucker isn't home! Motherfucker!* Taking a final swig of the cheap gin, you smash the bottle on the floor, your friends ducking the flying shards as you stumble away, flinging yourself back down the stairs. The rest of the night is a blur, but we can safely assume you made it back to your dorm room and fell asleep (god knows with whom or in what state of dress).

But wait: Mike stops by, late at night—surprise, surprise—wanting to check in on you, see you. You kiss, you clutch his thigh. He's tired, he just wanted to say hello, he returns to his own room. You go back to bed.

Saturday you wake late, and C stops by around eleven to go to brunch, but at this point it's practically lunch so you opt for a cheap burger. It's all you can afford anyway. You talk about how crazy, so fucking crazy, you all were last night. *What the fuck was that all about? Just blowing off some steam, that's all. No harm done. All good.* But you both agree to take it easy that night.

When evening rolls around, however, you find yourself back at the shitty little bar on State Street, even though it's not happy hour. You have your drinks, still with C, and you decide that this can be another one of your "heterosexual nights out." After three or four cocktails, you lurch out of the bar, and someone has the bright idea to get into C's car and go for a ride. You might as well own that this is *your* idea, though in retrospect you'll hardly call it one of your brightest. Especially when you remember that your idea is to go to K-Mart. Seriously. That's what you want to do. Go shopping at K-Mart. To her credit, C realizes she's too drunk to drive, so she hands you her keys, and you get behind the wheel with all the confidence of someone far too trashed to know better.

And here's the catch, the godalmighty catch: you don't even have a driver's license. You can't afford a car, so why get the license? That means you aren't insured. God help you, you poor sonofabitch. You're really fucked up. From this distance, I don't know if I feel ashamed of you or just pity your sorry ass. Likely both.

Anyway, you and C get in her car, you at the wheel, and you decide to peel out of the parking lot, totally forgetting that the first rule of driving while shit-faced is to *not* call attention to yourself. You head to K-Mart, which is on the other side of town, and you're so drunk, so fucking drunk, that you can barely see the road. It's dark, and your vision is so blurred (on top of the fact that it's not all that good to begin with) that you can only stay on the road by focusing on the dashed white lines in the middle of it. *Best not to go too fast*, you think, feeling smart. So you drive twenty or thirty miles an hour while cars zip around you, blaring their horns.

Miraculously, you make it to K-Mart and manage to park. The memories become blurry at this point, the alcohol sloshing around in your brain, but you stumble across a counter of cheap jewelry, and you and C buy yourselves the cheapest fake gold rings you can afford. They are so fucking tacky. But hey, it's heterosexual night out! You might as well get married, even if only for pretend. Somehow you get back to your dorm room, C returning to hers, and your lights are out before you can actually do any damage—to yourself, to C, to innocent bystanders or property.

Sunday comes, and you pile into someone's car with Mike, whom you haven't seen except for his brief late-night pop-in. Suddenly going to your parents' house feels like a *huge risk*, even though it's just for the parade, and even though your mother and father don't know anything about anything—that is, about who's sleeping with whom. You're half wondering if you might be exposing your parents to all of these folks—K and C and L and R and Mike, yes, even Mike—so they can put two and two together and come up with a three dollar bill. That might make whatever revelations you eventually attempt, if you attempt them, a bit easier. Perhaps. It's all so theoretical, even a bit theatrical. But you go and, of course, drink a little on the drive down to the city.

To make things still *more* interesting, you stop for gas at the station where a douchebag from the "other crew," the one that shot down your Homosexuality in Film proposal, works part-time. You want to sweep past him, ignoring him, delighting in your audacity, your Sunday outing *en masse* to a parade! What a queer group you are! You aren't bowed. You aren't cowed. You are queerly resilient. You are *fabulous*!

Shit, he's not here. But you can leave a message. An anonymous message. *Yeah, that's right!* You scribble a note—something along the lines of "Some homophobic turd better watch out or he's gonna get what's coming to him"—which, of course, you do not sign, and then hand it to the attendant, asking if he'll pass it along to "Dan." The crew is, as we used to say, in stitches, cavorting around the station and giggling with glee.

You get to the city, show up at your parents' house, tumble out of the car, make introductions, and spread out in the house already spilling over with guests who are going to use it as a base of operations, marching down to the parade and then back again for hot dogs and potato salad. Mother doesn't seem all that impressed with your friends; she doesn't like strangers. She warms up considerably when Mike looks out into the backyard and spots Clyde, your old basset hound, who is starting to forget you because you've been away at school for *so long*, at least in dog time. Mike sees the mottled mutt and says, Cajun lilt coming through, "Sha dog . . . oh, sha dog." *Sha* is how Cajuns pronounce *cher*, which isn't something you knew at the time, as your mother never taught you Cajun French. But she remembers the language of her youth, and she smiles broadly, face lighting up with recognition, with appreciation. Score one for Mike!

He wants to see your room, so you take him upstairs and make out on your bed, door closed, of course. Feels so transgressive, doesn't it, making out in your parents' house, your gay lover—say it: your *gay lover!*—sitting on your bed, leaning back, sliding his hand up your shorts, or is that *your* hand up *his* shorts? You're getting bolder, turned on by the proximity of so much condemnation, so much risk.

Then the parade, and the hot dogs and potato salad, and soon you are piling back into the car and headed back to Baton Rouge and class on Monday, and despite the alcohol, all the alcohol, you have a thought, an insight, an inkling that perhaps you should stop at the gas station and collect your threatening note. After all, is it actually a good idea to leave a threatening note? So you do, and wonder of wonders, the note is retrievable, and you feel rather proud of yourself, thinking ahead, doing the smart thing, even if it's the smart thing right after a pretty stupid thing.

But it's not smart enough, you soon find out. Not nearly smart enough.

"Good Thing
(Where Have You Gone?)"

FINE YOUNG CANNIBALS

The next morning, just as you're about to leave for class, the phone rings.

"Hello," you say, thinking it's K or another friend.

"Hello, is this Jonathan Alexander?"

"Yes," you say warily to the unfamiliar and strangely formal male voice.

"This is Officer X at the LSU Campus Police. A complaint has been filed, and we need you to come down to the campus station to discuss it. When can I expect you?"

At this moment, when something truly awful is in the process of happening—and, unfortunately, you've had the kind of life in which some pretty awful things have happened—you are quite literally beside yourself, as though you are looking at yourself from the outside. You are no longer in your body. You are splitting. You are becoming other—*I is an other*—but not the way you were hoping. Perhaps your mind is trying to get some remove from the situation, perhaps the better to think about it. Perhaps your mind is trying to flee the scene, escape the situation it has found itself in.

Je est un autre. No fucking shit.

"Can I come by this afternoon?"

"That will be fine. See you soon, Mr. Alexander."

You are still beside yourself. You are frozen, even as your body goes through its habitual motions: walk to class, sit in class, take notes, walk to another class, sit in class, take notes. Your future self (I, that is) imagines this is what you do because you will not remember anything until you are sitting across from the middle-aged bulky white cop in the LSU Campus Police station.

The officer, who isn't unpleasant, has you read a piece of paper that says something about you having the right to remain silent, the right to a lawyer, etc., etc. He won't reveal anything about what's going on until you sign, so you go ahead and sign, believing you have just destroyed your life. You start to consider suicide as a viable option. You are done. You are fucking done.

He then tells you someone has filed a complaint that you've been prank calling them.

You start to laugh. You quite literally laugh out loud.

The officer looks quizzically at you. This is not what he expected. It's not what you expected either; you expected something much, much worse. Drunken driving. Not remembered property damage. Not remembered bodily harm. Perhaps even something about vandalism (that broken gin bottle outside dear Matt's dorm room). But not this. No, not this. Oh, you're totally guilty. You've called a few people. No heavy breathing, nothing really creepy, but you've called Matt and others of the *bad* crew from the Film Committee and just hung up, trying to annoy them the way they've annoyed you. And that's what the complaint is about.

Your relief is indescribable.

For the cop, you spin out the story of your proposal and how it was voted down by a bunch of homophobes, who have likely filed this complaint to teach you a lesson. This is all just personal politics, bullshit from a group that doesn't like you, doesn't like your influence on the chair of the committee. The officer seems to buy it and says he'll refer the matter to the dean of students, as it doesn't really seem like police business. *But really*, he cautions, *watch yourself. Not to worry*, you assure him; you don't prank call and you don't intend to pick up the habit.

As you leave, you're not entirely sure that you haven't shit your briefs. You start to shake. You start laughing again, and a couple of approaching students move quickly out of your way.

That evening, when K and L and C come over, you all go out drinking, of course, and you tell them all about it. They're a little horrified that *the police* would be involved. They side-eye each other as they sip their cocktails.

Soon, you're drunk, again. Stupidly drunk. The girls escort you back to your dorm. When you all approach your door, you encounter a couple, a boy and a girl, headed upstairs. You are laughing and talking loudly. You notice the guy is cute.

"Well, hello there!"

The guy pauses and laughs, and there's more side-eye from your friends as you stumble toward him.

"Come on, Jonathan, into your room . . ."

"No no no no no, I want to stop and talk," you offer.

"Yeah, let him stop and talk," the guy says as his girlfriend urges him away; she doesn't think this will end well.

He's a big guy, though not tall. Stocky. Built. You go to put your arm around him, and your friends immediately step in between you and the dude.

"Nope, you're done."

"Aw, let him stay," the guy says, wanting to see where this might go, but someone has dipped into your pocket, fished out your keys, and opened the door. You're quickly ushered inside, and the couple continue on their way, the guy looking over his shoulder, smiling.

You collapse on your bed while your friends sit quietly around. You start to cry. And then you're sobbing as C moves toward you, cradling your head, gently rocking back and forth.

"He's crazy," K whispers.

"It's just the stress of it all," C offers.

"I dunno. . . ." K replies.

"I don't feel like I really know him. I mean, not really," L says.

And then they are gone. You don't see much of them anymore. For one thing, you don't return to the Film Committee. Attempts to get together will be halfhearted, and when they happen, things will feel strained. You don't see Mike again, not even in passing.

"If You Don't Know Me By Now" or "Right Here Waiting"

SIMPLY RED / RICHARD MARX

In time, you finish your thesis and graduate. Summa cum laude, with honors. On the strength of your academic record, you secure a position as teaching assistant in the LSU Program in Comparative Literature, in which you enroll as a graduate student. Your parents are *not* happy, though they will pay for none of it. They wanted you to teach high school, perhaps at the very school you attended, the place of so much abuse, so much suffering. *Nope*, you think. *Not me. Not ever.* You will have a stipend and be able to support yourself, finally. You enjoyed writing your honors thesis, when you weren't drinking and pining after a straight boy, and you think you'll focus on that kind of work for the time being—the writing, not the pining. Maybe one day you can teach college. Maybe write for a living. Who knows? In the meantime, there's a lot to learn.

The events of your senior year stay with you for a while. You feel their lingering pain. You numb these when you can. And that's how you find yourself on the floor of a friend of a friend's apartment, having blacked out the night before. You won't see much of these people again either. You're getting very good at burning through friends.

But come August, you'll go to graduate school and read and study and read and study. You'll make new friends. You'll even meet someone you'll marry. And while the Berlin Wall will start to crumble in November, signaling how a slow burn of dissatisfaction, how tremors of unrest can start to topple what once seemed so solidly and inexorably holding people back, you won't be so sure that your own walls are ready to come down. You tried. You really did. But not yet.

1993

"I Don't Wanna Fight"

TINA TURNER

You will always be surprised by what a difference a few years can make. You completed your BA in 1989, and now you are about to finish your PhD. Your teaching assistantship was for four years, and you desperately did *not* want to take out a loan—not to study comparative literature, already a ticket to unemployability—so you wasted no time. You committed to the relative impoverishment of graduate school so you could focus on your studies, though you picked up odd jobs here and there—one of which will become important in the course of this narrative.

But before we get to that, suffice it to say that 1993, like 1989, is a turning-point year for you. You often stop to wonder how every year is, each in its own way, a turning point, but some do stick out. It helps to have graduations to mark them—as well as items of historical note, such as the election of Bill Clinton, who becomes the forty-second US president on January 20 of 1993, followed on February 26 by the bombing of the World Trade Center (the first attempt to bring the towers down). At the time, these are just events that are happening in the broader world. They don't yet seem close to you and your world, your attention to politics perhaps less acute than it should be. You have, after all, been spending all of your time reading works of literature, and critical works *about* works of literature, and more immediately you've been reading and writing about nineteenth-century poetry, particularly the work of Walt Whitman, Arthur Rimbaud, and Gerard Manley Hopkins, the subjects of your dissertation. You've been casting your mind *back* more than not, focusing on these products of the past. Backward glances. The present could wait.

And indeed, in so many ways, the present *has* been waiting while you've sojourned in the halls of academe. You moved out of the barracks dorm into an off-campus apartment complex, suitably called Varsity Village, a conglomeration of brown buildings housing advanced undergrads, graduate students, and poverty-stricken assistant professors. (Your old philosophy professor lives just a few doors down, poor guy.) But as limited as your stipend is, you can afford the two-bedroom apartment—*sans* roommate—where you have moved all of your books out of your old bedroom in N'awlins and even augmented your collection through visits to junk sales and used bookstores. Secondhand furniture completes the look of lived-in student chic. Your friends actually envy you sometimes. You are proud. You are even, occasionally, happy.

You are also alone. Or, as you write in a poem from that year, "alone, but not quite lonely yet." (But, admittedly, close to lonely—otherwise, why protest that you aren't?)

After the difficulties of 1989, and the wake-up call of finding yourself on the floor of a stranger's apartment, having blacked out the night before, you have opted for sedation, more or less. Truth be told, what you've done is flee from your emerging queerness. You have run and hidden. You backtracked, backpedaled, just all-out fucking backed up and away from that hot mess—knowing enough to be thankful that you didn't drunkenly run a car off the road or over someone else and get kicked out of school to boot.

You are still a little scared. Scarred.

But you also want to tell the story of this time differently—not simply recast it in retrospect, which inevitably happens, and not just shine a better light on it and yourself, though that inevitably happens as well—

because it *was* different. A time of being scared, yes, and scarred, but also one full of interesting and new things. Not just your studies, which you generally enjoyed, but of new and interesting people.

Like the woman who will become your wife.

"Love Is"

VANESSA WILLIAMS AND BRIAN MCNIGHT

I stop here, because I need to figure out how to talk about your memories of Laura—Laura, who as of this writing is very much alive, whom I still very much respect, who will not be around much after you divorce but who will nonetheless help you change your life in ways for which you—and I—remain grateful. This kind of narration is inevitably one-sided, coming from one mind, one voice (however plural you feel yourself), and Laura always had—and has—her own take on things. You won't ever want to "set the record straight," telling the true and authentic version of your time together. You can't. We—you and I—can't. But we can allude and promise that, if the telling is foreshortened, it is out of regard for someone you will, in 1993, become legally wedded to. Someone who gets to tell her story for herself.

And no, it was not a mistake. It was love. It *is* love. It is 1993, and it is most definitely love.

Surprisingly enough, it began at the tail end of 1989. You're new to graduate school, taking things slowly, trying to stay out of trouble. You have also gone back to church, to the little Baptist church where you had originally been saved, having accepted the Lord Jesus Christ as your Personal Savior when you were a teenager, just before the demons of sex—of *homosexual sex*—started knocking at the door of your soul. You had let them in earlier that year. And they made a mess, a fucking mess. Not as bad as it could've been, however. You feel warned. You heed the warning. You respond to the call. You feel the twitch upon the thread, calling you home. And indeed, you are welcomed back. Folks are glad to see you. They missed you.

The prodigal returns, yadda yadda yadda.

You will forgive yourself this need for comfort, for the familiar, however toxic it is, however that twitching thread comes to seem, at times, like the noose around your neck. But you also recognize that you're increasingly on your own, your family not understanding what you're doing, your friendships from the Film Committee having fully dissolved, and other friends shying away too, frightened off by your out-of-control drinking. You need support. You find it the only place it seems to be offered, even if the offer isn't generous, coming as it does with a price. *Whoever wants to be my disciple must deny themselves and take up their cross and follow me.* You take up your cross. At least you're taking it up with others.

Despite the austerity of self-denial, there are some delights, and Laura is one of them—the roommate of one of your few remaining friends, Patty, a fellow Christian, someone you avoided much of last year, your senior year, because she would *not* have approved of your "lifestyle," but whom you cling to now. You attend campus lectures together. You study together, she working on her master's in library science. Safe. Even supportive. And then one night, at some event, she invites her roommate along, someone she'd been assigned to live with in the dorms.

Laura. Lovely Laura. Intelligent, attractive, energetic, a bit snarky. You like her immediately. You start spending time together, at first just as friends, then as more. Patty gets a little jealous—not that there was ever anything sexual between you and Patty, but she senses the interruption in your friendship, the turning of attention away from her and toward Laura. And Laura is *fun*. She's interesting. She's super smart. You take your meals together to enjoy each other's conversation. You go to the movies. You commiserate on your shared backgrounds, having both grown up in the New Orleans suburbs. You were once friends with a woman who grew up right across the street from Laura—the one who, during your freshman year, you cajoled into going to the gay bar down Highland. But you don't tell Laura that. That's all in the past. That's not something you need to return to. Not any time soon.

Herein lies the temptation, even now, to tell this story as though Laura were a wrong turn, a diversion on the one true queer path, so much more exciting but far riskier. But to give in to that temptation—to tell that story, already told so many times in so many ways by so many others—would be to ignore how much you needed Laura, needed the safety and security of that friendship and then, once you started making out (slowly, carefully), how much you needed—wanted—that intimate relationship. There is eros in comfort and security, not just in danger and risk. You will never condemn yourself for needing—for *wanting*—Laura, and when, years later, she asks for a divorce because there are other paths *for her*, calling *for her*, you will agree to it, but not because you want it. You won't. You'll want to keep going with her, perhaps opening up your relationship, allowing each other to explore alternative intimacies, different erotic entanglements, a bold and brave new world of polyamory. But that will be asking, perhaps, too much of both of you at the time, though you will often look back and wonder *what if?*

Ah, the failures of imagination, and the failure to act on even the limited imagination you have. You will forgive yourself those as well, eventually.

For now, though, you and Laura are having fun. Sedate and chaste fun, but that works for both of you. And then, two years into your relationship, she leaves for Boston, where she's attending graduate school. You drop her off at the airport the morning of her departure, having spent the night lying next to her in her bed, holding her, savoring your last moments, and then you're back in your car after walking her to the gate (when one could still do that sort of thing), and you're sobbing, tears streaming, great heaving cries of anguish.

You are bereft.

You spend the next two years talking on the phone when you can afford it (in the age before cellphones), seeing each other over holidays and at points during the summer, and on occasion flying to Boston to visit. You're otherwise studying, studying, studying, reading and writing seminar papers, preparing for your qualifying exams and then working on your dissertation. You write poems, sometimes about the half-life you have with her so distant. You feel split, part of you thousands of miles away.

If you have little more to say about this relationship, as significant as it is, as important as it will become, that's because so much of it is spent apart. And because you respect this woman, still. You always will. She deserves her privacy, her version, her story. You won't take that away from her.

But the part you have to tell, the part you can't *not* tell, is coming up . . . the part about the job you get at the same Mexican restaurant that Laura works at when she's in town. You have to tell that part, if only because it's where your queer story picks up again—or bits of it anyway, pieces you are always trying to make cohere, though you know that's almost always a mistake; telling a coherent story is something we only do for others. And coherence is never all that interesting.

You are about to become incoherent again.

"Right Here"

THE GRIND

You didn't know how much you'd enjoy working at the restaurant. Laura had been there, on and off, for years, especially during the summers, picking up shifts to make a little extra money, and you thought, *Why not? I'm home for the summer. Let's give it a shot.* As a way to ease yourself into this kind of work, you apply to be a host, smiling and greeting hungry guests, leading them to their tables—always *Right this way, please*, and never *Follow me*, the latter being too commanding, too imperative, not enough of an invitation. After all, we want to make our guests to feel *welcome. Sit a while. Have a margarita. Enjoy yourself. You are wanted here.*

You're surprised that you actually come to feel somewhat wanted here. Your coworkers, other hosts, the bussers, the kitchen folks—they're all roughly your age, all wondering what to make of their lives, what's even *possible* to make of a life in the early 1990s, the time of the Gulf War, Operation Desert Shield, because *This will not stand.* It's a time of war but in some ways feels so much like business as usual. For some, it is just business as usual: war profiteering amid the assault on democracy. Some of your coworkers served in the military, some have even been to Kuwait and Iraq. Sure, they are big and buff, the men, and the women might be smaller, but they are tough, tough as tacks. They look relatively unscathed, as though they'd just come back from a particularly intense summer camp. This will change, though you don't know that yet. In a few more years, from a few different wars, the bodies will return with the burdens of combat, the scars and absent limbs that are most definitely not from summer camp. But for now even those who have returned from war and serve chips and salsa alongside you—they speak of it as though it were far away, even though they'd seen it, if only from behind a screen.

What have *you* seen? Your own tough time, though admittedly of a different kind. But you got through it. Now, instead of slurping down those margaritas, you are serving them, bringing them to guests eagerly awaiting a little agave love. This feels normal. You are relieved to be doing something with your hands, with your body, walking briskly from host stand to table to kitchen to alert the next waiter that he or she is "sat," soon to be "in the weeds," running around frantically in the back of the house to check on food that's already five, ten minutes overdue while plastering on placating smiles. You love the excitement, the adrenaline, everything always moving so fast. You train to be a waiter, and soon you're raking in the tips. You find you can keep a lot of details in your head at one time—what folks are ordering, when it's going to appear in the kitchen window, how long the bar will take to make certain drinks, how quickly the busser is likely to clean up that table—so many details, all coming and going at different speeds, but you can do it. Sure, you're in the weeds at times, but isn't everyone at some point or another? And the cute busser will help you out because he knows you'll tip him a little extra. You develop your own tricks of the trade, not only to save time but to impress the guests. You never write anything down. The special orders for enchiladas and fajitas, the requests for the super hot sauce and the plea to not make it too too spicy—you hold all of that in your head, even for the six and eight and ten tops. And when the guests ask, "What happens if you forget something?"

"Well, then, you'll just get the wrong food."

Everyone laughs. *They laugh!* And in making these guests feel welcome, you are welcome in return. You belong here.

You had no idea anything could be like this. You'd never really worked in the world before. Not that you didn't want to. You begged your parents to allow you to get a job, any job, something for after school, something for a little extra money, something maybe to afford car insurance, or maybe even a car. But they always said, *Nope, not happening.* They needed you to work in your mother's nursery, her in-home nursery, helping her after school and throughout the summers, taking care of twenty-plus lovely darlings, screaming and crying and shitting their pants. You did. You served your time. And now that you're free, on your own, you can take the job you want, you can have that experience of the working world that had been denied you.

And you love it.

Even your mother recognizes this. At times, she and your father show up at the restaurant, occasionally with your sisters. Mother loves the chips. She leaves with big bags of them. She sees you enjoying yourself, being competent at something she can understand. She gets this work. She doesn't get your reading and writing, your English major and studies in comparative literature, whatever the fuck that is. But waiting tables? She approves. It's good, hard, honest work, the kind she's always done, the kind a working-class woman from rural Louisiana understands.

Maybe for the first time, you feel seen by her. And it's good to feel normal, finally, a little bit, after everything so far, especially after your senior year and the Film Committee and Matt and the drinking, etc.

It won't last.

"Deeper and Deeper"

MADONNA

Not only do you love the job, you also get to spend more time with Laura when she's home from Boston in the summer, and you really like the extra income. Your stipend only takes you so far, and tips become more than just pocket change; this is *legit* money. So even on the weekends during the school year, you often head back to town and pick up some shifts.

You start going out again, this time with your coworkers after your shifts—tentatively, at first—heading to restaurants open late, then bars. When Laura's in town, you all go out together, eat and drink with your fellow servers, and then the two of you head home, maybe to make out a bit, maybe to watch television at her parents' house before you call it a night and head back to your own parents' house. Nothing extreme. Pretty chill.

But Laura is gone for part of one summer, taking extra classes, and you're on your own. It's the middle of 1992, and you're working on your dissertation, which you need to finish before May, when your funding runs out. You're on a schedule, boy, and you know it. You're reading and notating and writing and reading some more. Things are moving. You're determined to finish this dissertation on Walt Whitman, Arthur Rimbaud, and Gerard Manley Hopkins—three major figures of nineteenth-century European poetics. Even though it's summer, you spend the days reading and writing, then you head to the restaurant for your evening shifts and then to another restaurant around midnight for a meal and then perhaps to a bar before crashing at 2 or 3 a.m., and then wake up around 9 or 10 to do it all over again. Sometimes, for a change of venue, you take your books uptown to PJ's Coffee, and in between reading and writing jags, you browse at the old Maple Street Book Shop. You feel swanky uptown, putting distance between you and your parents' shabby suburban home in Metairie.

On special nights, really special nights, you and your coworkers head to the French Quarter. You often limit your post-shift eating and drinking to nearby watering holes, everything relatively safe in Metairie. But sometimes, just sometimes, you all want something extra. Then it's thirty or so minutes downtown, to the Quarter. Bourbon Street. Live jazz. Pat O'Brien's and hurricanes. Strip shows. It's a whole other world. Year-round Mardi Gras. Contained, but completely out of control within those few square blocks.

You head down there in your car, maybe Janine or Erika or Nathan in tow, and you think of Arthur Rimbaud, a poet about whom you've been writing. The one with the older male lover, Paul Verlaine; the one who advocated for *le dérèglement de tous les sens*—the derangement of all the senses—as a way to open up new subjects for poetry, and new forms of writing for those subjects. Subjects such as, perhaps, homosexuality? Lots of drinking and some drugs, too. *Derangement.*

You understand the attraction. You, too, had your "season in hell," to borrow from one of Rimbaud's most famous poems, a tract that is all but a repudiation of his youthful attempts to pursue derangement. *But what the fuck?* you think. He was still a boy when he wrote *Une Saison en Enfer.* Shit, at twenty-four, twenty-five, you are older than Rimbaud when he *gave up* writing poetry, decided it was all fucking bullshit, and went off to Africa to become a gun runner, something real-world, consequential (however ethically suspect). You're not ready to give up yet. True, you're only really *writing* about the derangement of the senses, the opening up of new *poetic* content and forms, but you know, you *know*, some of what you speak. And walking down Bourbon Street, totally buzzed from those shots at Pat O'Brien's, you catch a whiff of your earlier days, your own season, your own flirtation with the dark side.

Maybe you aren't done with it just yet?

"Dreamlover" or "I'd Do Anything for Love (But I Won't Do That)"

MARIAH CAREY / MEAT LOAF

Strolling down Bourbon Street—catching glimpses of the frat boys rough-housing in their drunken stupors, groping one another, you imagining what will happen back at the house, pants fumbling down, paddles coming out, what to do with those pesky erections—you keep telling yourself that the past is past. While your fantasies haven't yet died, what's done is done; what happened during your senior year in Baton Rouge will safely remain there, like that saying about a trip to Las Vegas.

Done.

If only it were that easy. You're beginning to discover that in many, many ways, the past remains with you. Perhaps you're taken up with the nostalgia that any major transition is liable to generate. You're about to graduate—with a *PhD*, for chrissakes. You'll be done with school, you'll likely get married, you'll hopefully move away and start your life over, putting some actual physical distance between you and what you once almost became; so of course you are beset with reflections on what's gone before, in anticipation of the shadows cast by what's coming next.

There's a lot to think about.

It occurs to you that a counselor could help you sort things out. You're definitely influenced by Laura, who is studying for her master's in social work. She wants to be a therapist, likely working with the deaf, and as you've heard her talk about the benefits of therapy, of talking to someone about your "issues," you decide it couldn't hurt. Not that you feel a *huge need* to be helped. Your flirtation with the "dark side," with homosexuality, was just that, a flirtation—albeit one that could've ended in disaster. But who doesn't have such moments, who hasn't embraced a bit of the darkness within? Still, you're beginning to wonder if there's another story, perhaps another evil, lurking. And you owe it to Laura to make sure that whatever "issues" you have going into the relationship, increasingly looking like a marriage, are "issues" you are fully dealing with.

Get your shit together, you say to yourself. *Just get your fucking shit together.*

While you're making good money at the restaurant, nicely supplementing your teaching assistantship, you can't really afford a therapist. Lucky for you, the local chapter of Campus Crusade for Christ has free counseling. Given your recent rapprochement with Christianity, it's a viable option. If you don't like it, you won't have to go back and you won't be out any cash, so what the hell?

There's a catch, though: what do you tell this Christian counselor? You can't go in there and say, "Gee, I thought I was gay, even fooled around with a guy during my year of debauchery, but I also really want to get married. Oh, and I still fantasize about spanking plump boys' butts." Nope. You'd be ushered out immediately, cast into the flames where there is weeping and gnashing of teeth. They won't want your kind anywhere near them.

There are stories you could tell, feelings you could reveal, but you don't have an answer to the question you're facing: *why did you sin in those particular ways?* You don't have a handy explanation. At least, you don't think so. You aren't entirely sure. But as you search yourself, you slowly realize there are some dreams, some murky images. You are watching a movie, a dark blue screen with an eerie, overly sweet Chopin waltz playing on the piano, softly, as shadows move over the screen. What are they doing? What *are* they doing? You are uneasy. The shadows, none quite assuming any recognizable position, nonetheless evoke thoughts and feelings, not quite urges, but something . . . something.

Then it hits you. You were abused as a child. You were *sexually* abused. Molested, they call it. And the Chopin, that's a clue, a *big* clue. It was likely your uncle. He *loved* classical music. That's where you would've heard the waltz. And the shadows, the dark blue—those are the images left on the backs of your eyelids as you closed them in terror, as you must have closed them in sheer terror when it was happening, the abuse, the molestation, so you wouldn't see the atrocities and abominations being inflicted on your young flesh. *Squeeze those eyes tight, boy. This will all be over soon.*

Except it isn't. It isn't over. You've been left with the scars, with the profane desires, the perverse impulses, the twisting of the natural and straight course of your development as a sexual being. After all, who really gets off on being spanked, on being punished, *on being tied up and abused?* Only someone who is fucked up, *someone who has been fucked up.*

Could this be it? The reason for my darkness? Uncle Glen abused me. That's why I am the way I am. It's not my fault.

It's not my fault. . . .

"I Have Nothing"

WHITNEY HOUSTON

So: what *really* happened?

You don't actually know. And it's that lack of knowledge that opens up the space—or allows a space to be opened up within you—to tell your story in such a way that you do not bear full culpability for your feelings, your desires.

What you *do* know is that you had an uncle, Glen, your mother's brother, the only one of her relatives who actually lived in New Orleans, the only nonimmediate family member you got to know as a child, because he lived close enough for your family to see on a regular basis. Perhaps due to this, a limited sample size, he ended up being your *favorite* uncle. Though in retrospect there are many more reasons.

He was a big man, burly, and fun. A good old Cajun boy with touches of sophistication. With his jeans and flannel and mustache, he was what in the 1970s would have been called a "gay clone," but the look worked for him. Today, you'd call him a queer hipster lumberjack, just in a big boy's body. Not fat. Someone who would twirl you around, roughhouse with you, but gently enough, and he'd bring over his big dogs, boxers, their energetic natures delighting your childhood spirit as they bounced around while the grown-ups talked.

But more: this big burly fun uncle encouraged your habit of reading, buying you a subscription to *National Geographic*, a set of Funk and Wagnalls encyclopedias, and even a bookcase to house them. He loved that you started reading Tolkein at a young age. He nurtured your sense of the fantastic. You loved going to his home in the French Quarter, in part because everything in the Quarter was, even to a young boy, far more exotic and interesting than in the suburbs. He lived in a long house, what's called a shotgun house, with room after room after room leading back to a secret urban garden. He loved having dinner parties, inviting over friends and family to feast in the elegantly outfitted dining room at the front of the house, but only after having wine and *hors d'oeuvres* in the garden, large bushes and ferns creating a private and sheltered space. Moving from one end of the house to the other, you had to pass through his bedroom, perhaps the most fantastic room of all, in which large sheets had been suspended in folds from the ceiling, creating a cloudy canopy strung with white christmas lights. You could imagine sinking into his waterbed, surrounded by fluffiness and yellow light, a divine cloud of rest, comfort, security.

With whom did he share that bed? With Michael, his partner, a schoolteacher. Glen worked for the phone company. They had a good life. A life full of friends and pleasures. Oh, and the music, the music. Glen loved classical and had a large reel-to-reel sound system on which he'd play lush orchestral scores. When you yourself started listening to classical music at twelve or thirteen, the first album you bought was Herbert von Karajan's recording of Beethoven's Symphony No. 6, "Pastoral," with its charming melodies and climactic thunderstorm in the middle! You couldn't wait to call up Glen and tell him. He loved it. You think he must have loved you too. You wonder if he saw in you a potential kindred spirit, another sexual outlaw, a budding pervert, a little gay boy. A queer. A *faggot*.

You wonder that in 1993 as you remember the Halloween costume he made you one year, when you were barely pubescent—an outfit with sequins and mirrors sewn into it, with a huge black cape. Imagine a drag queen Darth Vader. One fall evening, Glen and Michael brought it to the house for you to try on, and your parents said, *Nope, no, not going to happen. It was, uh, too much.* And then earlier memories, Glen visiting your mother, likely his favorite sister just as he was likely her favorite brother—the only one besides her who moved from Cajun country to the Big City, the City That Care Forgot, so they could both find other lives, perhaps other loves not available to them in rural southwest Louisiana. He would visit, and they would talk, and you would play off to the side, a boy of five or six, still in your underwear, running around in your tighty-whities, and he'd catch you and hold you and slip an ice cube down the back of your briefs. You'd squeal with delight, and even now your butt cheeks clench a little bit—but is it with the pleasure of memory, a fond memory, or do your cheeks clench with the recollection of something darker, something more sinister, the ice cube evoking hot sensations of shame, perhaps even of violation?

Then back even further, maybe a year or two: Glen and Michael taking you to see *Fantasia* one evening. All you really recall is wanting to leave early. And then . . .

Then, nothing. A blank.

Years later, you sit crying in your parents' kitchen, telling them that you've been in counseling. You've been grappling with . . . with . . . you can't get it out, but your father can.

"I think I know. You're homosexual," he says.

You freeze. You stop crying. His tone is dispassionate, factual, but it's shocking nonetheless to hear him say the words. You thought he wasn't paying attention, that he didn't *care* to pay attention, but he's found you out. *He knows.* Even your cold, disengaged father knows. Finally, you recover enough to say, "Well, you're close. I think I was molested by Uncle Glen."

Your parents fall silent. You have surprised them after all. A painfully awkward moment passes, then another. You've accused your mother's favorite brother of something horrific. Will they believe you? Shout denials? Accuse you of lying? And then one of them, you'll forget which, or perhaps both of them, brings up that night Glen took you to see *Fantasia*.

Apparently you had called after the movie, the aborted movie, wanting to come home, *crying to come home*. But your parents were out on a date and told you to stay with Uncle Glen.

"That must have been it," they say. "That must have been when it happened." Despite their outward calm, you sense their relief—the same relief you are feeling. You have offered them an explanation for you, for why you are the way you are, and they have seized upon it. *And Glen*, you imagine them thinking, *of course*. Of course he was capable of it. He was a homosexual; a deviant.

You've never been so glad to have something as awful as the sexual molestation of a child—*your sexual molestation as a child*—be confirmed, or at least be as confirmed as it could be.

This is, after all, the story you've been piecing together with the counselor from Campus Crusade for Christ, a gentle, kind, early-middle-aged man who treats you with respect, who recognizes that none of this is your fault, who understands, who assures you that God himself understands.

"It's all going to be okay," he tells you. "God will take care of this."

And yes, it seems that god *is* taking care of this. God himself has had your parents confirm what you suspected. And they are sorry too, so sorry. They should've picked you up. They really should have.

At the time, the early '90s, such stories are easily believable. There've been a rash of similar testimonies, recovery of lost memories and buried traumas, of newly exhumed violations. People are going to jail for the atrocities they committed but that were forgotten by their victims because the pain, the pain of it all, was just too great for a child's body and mind to bear. But memories come back, apparently. And just because your memories aren't coming back, just because you don't remember *precisely* what happened, that doesn't mean there's not enough to go on . . . to piece together the right kind of story for your current needs.

Moreover, your uncle can't refute what you've said. He died when you were thirteen, just after the fiasco with the failed Halloween costume. He'd been suffering from multiple myeloma for some years, and his body finally succumbed to the cancer. 1982. You saw him in his hospital bed, his last bed, his death bed—brought in to say hello while his brothers and sisters crowded around in the hospital lobby, awaiting the inevitable. He was shaking, almost violently. He didn't want to die.

But he did. Because that's the appropriate end for someone like him. Even his longtime companion, Michael, was largely absent by that point, tired of caring for someone terminally ill. See? Abandoned by his "lover." Sad, pathetic homosexuals. They're getting what they deserve. And just a few years later, when AIDS is everywhere in the news, you'll wonder: was it really cancer? That emaciated body, splotched, bruised . . . Your relatives, your cousins, will wonder. They will wonder and ask you, especially after they find out about you, that you too are gay. After all, you'll know, right? You should know. *Do you think it was AIDS?*

Who can tell? Glen isn't telling. He's not saying *anything* now. And that's the point. He can't defend himself.

You are more than relieved. You almost feel that you've earned this. The story makes sense. Everything fits.

"Runaway Train"

SOUL ASYLUM

But it doesn't. There are lingering doubts. You are uneasy with your story, the narrative that you so desperately want to make sense. Ultimately, you'll never know what happened that night of *Fantasia*, and maybe that's okay. Maybe nothing happened, nothing at all. Just because you can't remember doesn't mean something either good *or* bad occurred.

A couple of decades later, when you are talking with your mother—your mother who moves in with you, your last parent, the one you'll care for in her old age—she'll tell you the stories of her younger life, and Glen's life. Slowly at first, and with more detail over time, she'll reveal how her alcoholic father was sent to the state penitentiary for too many DUIs. But before then, how he'd come home drunkenly raging, throwing against the wall food her mother had spent all day preparing. A few specifics, bits and pieces, and you start to fill in the rest. How Glen needed to get the fuck out of there, how he'd been abused, how he'd been beaten for being a sissy boy, how he'd wrap his big burly self around him for protection. How he moved to New Orleans (with your mother, something of a tomboy, a gender outsider herself) to get away from the rural backwardness, from those who would rather beat a faggot than learn how to love him. How Glen would find and build a community, find something of love, find something of a survivable life, until he couldn't survive it anymore.

He was the only uncle you really got to know, and he'd been taken away right as you were forming your own particular interests, becoming pubescent enough to get a glimpse of your own queernesses . . . when you could've used a gay father figure, someone who understood. He was taken away right before you really started to need him.

Hearing these stories of his early life, and remembering what you *do* know about him from your own experience, you will feel shame—shame that you needed a narrative of abuse. Shame that you betrayed him, your possible gay father figure. Shame that you sacrificed your memory of him—and your parents' as well—because you so needed not to feel the things you were feeling, not to desire the things you were desiring.

Boy, you will look back on all of this—from the mess of the Film Committee to the betrayal of your uncle—and you'll wonder how you survived. But that's what all of this is about, isn't it, including the narrative you piece together in 1993? You are trying to survive. Others who didn't grow up as you did, in that time and place, won't be able to fathom what it was like. You hope this story helps them understand.

You also hope their lives are such that they never truly *can* understand.

"I Will Always Love You"

WHITNEY HOUSTON

And what about your *real* father, the one who, when you sat down to talk about yourself, your thoughts of marriage, your trauma—the one who guessed, before you said anything, that you were, in fact, homosexual? What about him? He occupies so little of the story thus far. Are you withholding? And if so, what?

He must be more than just a bit player, this father of yours, someone who appears at times to fulfill a perfunctory role, perform a predetermined script. But perhaps that's all that was really there. Perhaps that's all he ever was: a performer. Someone handling an obligation, biding time, going through the motions, otherwise not engaged, not going out of his way to deliver lines with any extra gusto or aplomb. Just *Dad*. Or, as the script would have it: *The role of the father as played by Henry Alexander, a walk-on part, with minimal lines, a few guest appearances, someone barely present and rarely affecting the dramatic arc of the narrative.*

Is that fair? Even after all these years, is that a fair assessment, an appropriate review of his performance?

Funny how the metaphor can get away from you in its tracing of the curves and contours of a life lived. Your father *like* a bit actor playing his part. But what if that's not a metaphor?

And can you know that? Can you know that that is how he saw fatherhood? So much of what you *do* know is what you *don't* know.

You don't know how to tell the story of your father except as an absence. Even he knew this about himself. One of your most striking early memories of him is of the family—you, your sisters, your parents—sitting in a pizza parlor on a hot and sticky Saturday. You must be ten. You eat, they eat. As usual, not much talking. Then a song comes on the radio, an oldies station, the Beatles' "Got to Get You into My Life." Your father laughs, a rare thing—he *laughs*, saying, "That's what he must sing about me." He's gesturing to you, already knowing that, at ten, you're not much a part of his life, just as he's not much a part of yours. You're too young at the time to be hurt, to be outraged. But you will remember. The hurt and outrage will come later.

Perhaps that is one of the primary reasons you gravitate toward Glen—because there was something, a connection, a memory, even a possibility. You might have ultimately gotten things wrong, you might be botching and butchering his story as you're telling it. But there's at least a story to be told.

Not so with your father.

Oh, you'll try. In your thirties, you'll write and then publish a piece about him, pretentiously titled "Fourteen Ways of Seeing Dad." Just a few years after the revelation in the kitchen, you'll write this, wanting to know what his life was like, what brought him to the silences he surrounded you with, what might have prompted him to hazard that you were, indeed, homosexual.

Had he dealt with the same desires? In your piece, you will fill out scenes in his life, such as this one, which you believe you heard somehow, somewhere—but when, where? In the piece you write, your father tells this tale to the family one night, just after Mother clears the dinner plates:

Coming home from the army, honorably discharged from his forced service during the Korean War, he's hitchhiking home on a dusty road in Georgia. A convertible pulls up, top down, and a youngish guy tells him to get in. He can take Dad as far as Birmingham, possibly farther. Your dad gets in, and they drive for hours and hours.

Eventually, they stop at a motel to spend the night. The driver takes the bed, and Dad spreads out on the floor. The lights are turned off, and after a moment, the driver tells your dad that he would probably be more comfortable in the bed. Your dad agrees and climbs in beside him.

You don't know why, but you imagine your dad doing this very carefully—not in a fearful sort of way, but in a methodical, almost gingerly manner. Quietly. A few minutes pass, and then the driver puts his hand on Dad's thigh. Immediately, your dad gets out of bed, pulls on his clothing, and leaves the hotel.

You imagine him walking all night. Somehow, he eventually arrives home in Mississippi. Picayune.

You don't know what he told the driver as he left the motel, can't conceive of what they must have talked about for the hours they were together, crossing Georgia and Alabama. They may not have said much at all. Dad spoke very little.

In your telling, you and your sisters remain quiet and still when he stops speaking, while mother washes the dishes. No one knows what to say, but you, at fifteen, understand the story has been for your benefit, a cautionary tale. You get up and walk quietly away from the table.

But you didn't learn that story from him, did you? Maybe your mother? Where does it come from? Under what circumstances were you told this? And why?

Why are you retelling it?

Another scene, this one clearly made up, a concoction of your imagination:

Your father plans his escape. He's twenty-five, maybe twenty-six, and he senses that time is running out. He would like to travel West, destination unsure, but he knows there is something in the world he can do, something he can put his hands to besides the jars of jelly he helps fill, or the meters he detaches from the homes of those who refuse to pay their bills.

He won't go alone, but Beau, his best friend, this funny, funny Black man from Lafayette, refuses to go with him. Beau has friends here. More importantly, he has family, and they would never forgive him leaving the state. They barely forgave him moving to New Orleans, but in the course of a life, some things must be done.

So your dad and Beau argue about it one summer evening. Beau offers him the necessary cash, a friendly consolation prize, but your dad is not appeased. There are some minor accusations, nothing really serious, but the two don't speak again like they used to. Beau finds other friends. Your dad works at his job.

Then he gets married.

You, too, will get married. And in the future, as you write this scene, you will already know that these stories are not about your father. They are about you. They are always about you. Not just because that's how writing works, but because that's how your relationship with your father works. You fill in the void with yourself, imparting to him your imaginings, your desires, your futures—because there's otherwise nothing there. There's no *there* there at all.

"In the Still of the Night (I'll Remember)"

BOYZ II MEN

Like everyone else, you are thrust into the middle of another's story. Your mother's, your father's, your uncle's, Laura's—all of you doing the best you can to make your way through the presences and absences, the heres and theres and everywheres and nowheres of your narratives.

The days pass. In one of them you return from your meeting with the counselor whom you made complicit in the story that gives you cover, that provides you an excuse, that makes a *there* there for why you feel the way you do, why you fantasize at times about boys, why you whip your own ass, punishing your body for what it wants (or at least, at the time, that's what you tell yourself you're doing).

You get back to your apartment, the well-outfitted apartment with the spare bedroom, your office, shelves lined with books, the large white desk on which you write your dissertation, the apartment that is the envy of your friends. You have people over for cocktails—made-up drinks like Derridean Delight (a sickly sweet mix of cheap rosé, cheap vodka, and sugary lemonade)—watch VHS tapes of obscure foreign films, and play Samuel Barber's Adagio for Strings, which makes your Christian friend Henry cry. (You enjoy making Henry cry.) And then your friends, fellow graduate students, leave the apartment, everyone a bit tipsy, and you strip down to your briefs and t-shirt and continue drinking, the blush wine still strong in your veins, getting stronger. You dance around the room, dance in your underwear, dance to the hum of rosé in your veins, and you think of poetry, the poetry you're writing about, the poetry you're writing, the poetry you love, such as William Carlos Williams's "Danse Russe":

. . .

if I in my north room
dance naked, grotesquely
before my mirror
waving my shirt round my head
and singing softly to myself:
"I am lonely, lonely,
I was born to be lonely,
I am best so!"
If I admire my arms, my face,
my shoulders, flanks, buttocks
against the yellow drawn shades,—

Who shall say I am not
the happy genius of my household?

You know what he's talking about, you *know* (you've taped a photocopy of this poem to the wall above your bed), and you *dance dance dance*, flexing your buttocks in your briefs, running your hands up and down the sides of your body, past your slim waist, down your butt, across your thighs, the shades of your apartment drawn though you peek out of them sometimes to see if anyone is there, if anyone is watching, the lonely, lonely genius of your household.

Your favorite part is the opening of the poem—

If I when my wife is sleeping
and the baby and Kathleen

are sleeping

. . .

—because you know, somehow you already know, that this is the future, even if her name isn't Kathleen, even if there isn't a baby, though the counselor has promised one. He has spoken for god himself: there will be a child, god will give you a son, all will be right with the world, all will be right with *you*. But you understand that what will be right will be the moments you strip down to your underwear and dance around the room, flexing your buttocks, your wife and child asleep. You are lonely, lonely, and you are best so.

You drain the glass of wine and head to your room, not the one that serves as your office—the dissertation will be waiting for you in the morning—but your bedroom, where a couple of thick mattresses rest directly on the floor. You go to the closet and rummage for a box, a secret box, one with "supplies," as you put it: old belts, some rope, a pole or two with metal hooks.

You align the poles between the mattresses, one at the top of the bed, the other at the foot, their hooks sticking out. You take some belts and wrap one around your right ankle, then the left, buckling them tightly, then roping them to the hooks, so your legs stretch wide across the lower part of the mattress. Lying down, you sink into the bed, arch your back as your legs strain against their bonds, rubbing your hands up and down your sides and across your buttocks, swatting yourself once, then again. Your erection starts to strain against your tighty-whities, but you don't touch it, you don't touch it.

Tying your arms down is harder, but you've done this before and know how to manage it. You wrap one belt, then another around your wrists, cinching them tight and looping more of the rope through metal hooks at the top of the bed. Then, holding the slack in your hands, you pull, pull, pull, stretching your wrists across the bed, the rope around one belt being pulled by the opposite hand. You've already looped knots that you yank tighter and tighter until your arms, like your legs, are stretched across the mattress, and you are spread-eagled, trapped, bound, at the mercy of . . . admittedly at your own mercy, but yes, at the mercy of something, at the mercy of your past and your future, of everything that has happened, of everything that will happen, of everything you've done, of all that you will not do. You're ready to be victimized. You're a victim-in-waiting, someone to whom something is about to be done—or at least that's the fantasy.

As crazy as self-bondage might seem to someone who isn't a practitioner, you're not stupid. While the knots are tight, they are simple ones, shoelace knots, something a child could do and undo. With a little effort, you can easily wriggle free, but you love the moment when you think you might not be able to, when you think it might be *too* tight, that you might actually have fucked up, have fucked yourself up. There's a panic, a moment of panic, but it subsides: you see the slack, you can get out—*it's ok, it's going to be ok.* But for a moment you *want* to be trapped, to feel yourself helpless, to know yourself doomed, *fucked*, and your erection grows, pushing against the cotton fabric holding it in check. You twist and squirm, arching your back as much as you can, rolling from side to side within the limits of your bonds, and then the wriggling and bucking and straining settles into a rhythmic throb, an up and down pulse, a steady movement as you find the sweet spot, the tip of your cock rubbing against the elastic waistband of your briefs, back and forth and back and forth until you explode in your underpants, your toes quivering, your breath exhaling in almost a shout. . . .

You fall back into the mattress, relaxing your pull against the restraints. Your breathing stills. You close your eyes. You rest, rest, for half an hour, maybe more. In time, you rouse and loosen the bonds. You aren't trapped after all. You can escape. And that is its own kind of relief, its own release. You put away the supplies, peel off your sticky briefs and put them in the bag you'll take home tomorrow so your mother can wash them, wash all your clothes while you are at the restaurant working your shift.

"Do You Believe in Us"

JOHN SECADA

For two years, Laura has been mostly in Boston, studying for her master's in social work. You miss her. All the time. You talk on the phone once a week, usually Thursday evenings while you're still in Baton Rouge. But on Fridays you're often heading home to New Orleans, where you work in the restaurant all weekend long. You're young. Your body can take it: teaching your class and writing your dissertation Monday through Friday, then waiting tables Friday night, Saturday night, and hosting on Sunday. You're making money. You're writing. You're loving your class. You are alone, but not quite lonely yet, or at least you're *lonely, lonely* in that William Carlos Williams way that is best so. And you've got your story, the narrative is set, you know what you're about, what the past was about, what your depraved and perverted feelings are about, and it's good, all good. You can plan for the future, move ahead. You can get married. Life will go on.

All good. Everything is good. And then you meet Ethan.

How will you describe Ethan in the future? Is he the loose thread that shows how easily everything could unravel? Is he the blight, the moldy spot on an otherwise totally edible slice of bread? Is he the blemish that mars the beautiful face, something more damaging than the imperfection of a beauty mark?

There is an unfairness in such descriptions, a failure to capture the complexity of what Ethan's presence means in your life. The loose thread, the moldy spot, the marring imperfection—none of them comes close to capturing your sense of the inevitability of him, of what he comes to signify for you. And even that is overstated, hyperbole for a non-relationship that you won't think much of in time, years from now, but that in the moment will seem everything to you.

Some context. First, there's the restaurant, its own microcosm, the waiters and bussers and kitchen staff who come and go but also the ones who, steady state, keep showing up for their shifts. The tall blond with the gorgeous voice who might, just might, want to be an opera singer. The boys returning from the Gulf War, no real combat experience but twitchy and beautiful for having been that close to unspeakable violence. The druggies—kids who work to maintain their habits. One of them (so cute, so very very cute in his busser outfit of tight black pants and red shirt, with wavy black hair and piercing eyes) is always chatting you up. He wants to get high with you, and you think about it, you're thinking about it. . . . Where could this go? What might happen if the two of you lie in bed together and smoke some pot, chilling? You don't do it. You can't; it's too close to danger. But he asks. *No pressure, man. No pressure, just chillin'. It's all good.*

And then Ricky, *obviously* gay, short, lithe, studies ballroom dancing, unsure what he wants to be when he grows up but is enjoying himself now, flitting around the restaurant, and you mean no derogation when you say flitting, because that really describes how he moves through space—lightly dancing from room to room, kitchen to main dining room. And he's friendly, so friendly, always ready with a good word, a kind comment, or a snarky tidbit if you're open to that sort of thing. He also works at a photo-processing store, developing rolls of film and making extra copies of the naked pics that men and their girlfriends take. He's got a stash of these that he keeps in his car, and he enjoys showing them off at work. You sneak a peek or two, more shocked than titillated that someone would create a personal archive of other people's, of *strangers'*, nakedness.

99

But good on him, you guess, for pursuing his desires, or at least for knowing what he wants, however invasive it might be of others' privacy. He's found a way to survive. You're not in the least attracted to him.

Ethan, though . . . Ethan is another story. He starts as a busser and then moves to the wait staff, his buff frame navigating the small passages between tables, his plump but not fat butt straining against his black uniform pants. Of course you notice his butt, his behind, his *derrière*. But not just that. He's got quite the head of blond curls, closely cropped. He's pale, but his broad shoulders, built arms, and muscular legs (also straining against his pants) signal health, even vigor. He's strong. Manly. He horses around with the male servers. He flirts with the female servers. He talks sports. He's eager to get a drink after work, always in a group, a laughing group of grubby servers having ended their shifts and closed the restaurant, who are wanting a bit of diversion before heading home and crashing. He's a guy's guy, a generally pleasant and affable human being.

You quickly come to hate his guts.

Of course, that's far from the truth. But a part of you, a part that you can't articulate fully yet, resents the ease with which he seems to move through the world—the bonhomie, his easy fraternity with other men. You don't have that. For sure, you're hardly disliked at the restaurant. You do go out with the crew at times. But not the way Ethan does. His presence reveals the extent to which you are, in many cases, a tagalong, someone invited as part of the larger group but not someone others are actively seeking out, with whom they are making particular plans. You all go out, but often enough there are splinter groups, breakaways, subsets—and they tend to cluster around Ethan. People *like* Ethan, because, well, he's easy to be around. What you see is what you get. You—you are not like that. And while no one would accuse you of outright dishonesty or deception, you can't help but wonder if they perceive something *amiss* about you, something not fully forthcoming. Something a bit *off*. Just like they did in high school, even if now, at the restaurant, everybody a bit older, no one is throwing a stone at you: outcast, unclean.

So you resent Ethan while at the same time your eyes are drawn to his muscular bottom, his tightly kinked blond curls, his bulging biceps, his piercingly pale blue eyes. (Shades of Matt!) He's friendly and attractive. You enjoy chatting with him. Your gaze lingers on him as you sit in the group after work at dinner or at a bar. But not for long, never for too long. You don't want to make it weird. You know better. You've been raised to avoid giving too much attention to the boy you like. So you writhe and seethe inside when Ethan leans over to his friend, the fellow server quickly becoming his best mate, and puts him in a headlock, tousling his hair, joking about how he can't lift, how much more Ethan can bench-press than he can. They work out together; of course they do. They're developing a separate friendship, a whole *life* beyond the group. Beyond you. Why are you not part of it? Why couldn't Ethan have chosen you? Why can't Ethan playfully put *you* in a headlock? How good that would feel. How even potentially *healing*. Yes, that's right: you think, *healing*. You'd experience some male companionship, some real male friendship, some male *bonding*. That's what you need. It's not a *son* you need, as the Christian counselor suggested. What you need is a *friend*. A *male friend*. A buddy, a bro, a "boy," which is how the guys refer to their male friends: "my boy."

You decide to strategize. You can do this. You can make this work. You'll invite Ethan out with just one or two others, two young women who work at the restaurant, but women you don't think Ethan is interested in. You don't want competition for his attention. It would be completely counterproductive—an outright *disaster*—if Ethan paired off with one of them on your, uh, friend date. After all, the women are only invited because it would be too weird to ask Ethan out *just the two of you*. But this group, a modified group, seems like a safe place to start.

You'll remember this night for some time to come. You, Ethan, Jasmine, and . . . well, the other girl can't make it. So just the three of you. Even better, especially since Jasmine is *definitely* not Ethan's type. Nope. *This will be great*, you think.

The three of you finish your shift, already having agreed to head out together, in a smaller group for a change. That part was surprisingly easy. You each spend a little time in the staff bathrooms, changing your clothes, washing off. Primping. Yes, Ethan is a primper. He spends time . . . doing whatever he does to prepare himself for an evening out. You suspect he's a little vain, and truth be told, it's one of the things about him you make fun of to the other wait staff. *Spending all that time in the bathroom? Must be masturbating—to his own reflection! Hey, cut him some slack: he's got to spend all that time primping just so we can stand to look at him!* Poor Ethan, but he's a good sport. He can take it. And his being such a good sport is one of the things that makes you hate him a little. You're jealous. You are. But only because you want his attention, the attention he doles out so generously to others. Well, he can dole some of it out to you tonight. You pile into Jasmine's car as she's agreed to, well, not exactly be the designated driver, but to "watch herself." This is New Orleans. You can't expect the driver not to partake. But you know Jasmine. She's a little bit older, like late twenties. She's not stupid. It'll all be good. So off you go, everyone singing along to the radio as opposed to talking, except for the *de rigueur* stories about the craziest tables you had that night, the cheapest tippers, those lousy fucks, etc. Work talk and singing, work talk and singing, gossip, gossip, gossip—a typical start to an after-work night out.

Of course, you wind up on Bourbon Street. The French Quarter. Why the fuck not? It's a Saturday night. And while there are other bars closer to the restaurant, closer to home, this is where you go if you're young and have cash to spare. To get still more cliché, you all decide to hit up Pat O'Brien's, the famous bar on Bourbon that serves hurricanes, the drink of damage, the concoction of catastrophe, a sugary sweet mix of rum and juice. You can't fully succumb to stereotype, however, so you order a pousse-café, which Wikipedia will tell you later is a "cocktail in which the slightly different densities of various liqueurs are used to create an array of colored layers, typically two to seven." At the time, you think it's something particular to Pat O's, but it's just something the bartender talked you all into because you looked like you could afford it. And for tonight, you can. Your shift was good. The tips came in, and you're feeling it, feeling it. You've got your friends, and the object of your potential affection—fraternal affection, buddy, bro. Let's get hazed, bro!

And, boy, do you. The pousse-café is . . . special. Tomorrow you will remember, vaguely, having two of them. And so does Ethan. Jasmine has just one, because that's the responsible thing to do. You're talking, talking, laughing loudly, everyone having a good time. You won't recall much of the conversation, but everyone is smiling, smiling, Ethan clapping you on the back, one of the guys, all good fun, good fun, and Jasmine too. It's cool, all cool.

And then . . . some group of ratty frat-boy-looking motherfuckers comes up and starts talking to Ethan, some guys who all used to go to school with him, and they're standing over the table, clustered around your boy, and they're not paying any attention to you and Jasmine, no attention at all. What the fuck?

Jasmine can sense that you're put out, so she suggests a change of venue. Another bar, you know, something a little less crowded? Ethan's in. And so are the new boys. Fuck.

Ethan and his friends head out, and—whoops!—you nearly fall over as soon as you stand up. Pousse-café! The already dark room blurs, as though the bar and then Bourbon Street are suddenly submerged beneath the muddy waters of the Mississippi, just a few blocks to the east. But no, the only thing submerged is your brain, in layers of liqueur. And maybe your heart. Bitter, but just a little. The alcohol numbs a lot of what you're feeling.

Numbs, that is, until you're out on the street, deep into the night, revelers already dwindling but still a healthy crowd of drunks, folks milling about, intoxicated, like you and Jasmine and Ethan looking for the next restaurant or bar. And his boys, of course. You haven't even caught their names. You don't care.

And then you're sitting down, right in the middle of the street. Down. Ethan and the others walk on ahead, and Jasmine starts laughing, pulling at your arm. "Get up, asshole! Get up!" You start laughing, too, laughing at Ethan walking away.

Jasmine squats beside you. "What's up, dude? What the fuck?" Hard words, but she's smiling.

"Oh man, oh man. I'd totally do him. I really would."

She stops smiling, blinks. Points to the boys. "Ethan?"

"Yeah. I really would."

"Oh dude, I don't think he swings that way. I mean, I get it. But I don't think that's going to happen."

And she's right. You know she's right. It would be cliché to say that this has all been a mistake, but that's precisely what runs through your head. It's all been a mistake. A huge mistake. You shouldn't have come. You shouldn't even have suggested this. What were you thinking? Seriously, what were you thinking?

"I know, right? What was I thinking?"

You get up, Jasmine pulling on your hand, then helping you walk down Bourbon, arms linked, heads leaning together. You catch up with Ethan, and Jasmine says that she thinks it might be time to go home; she's a bit tired, long night and all.

Ethan says he can get a ride back with the boys as he high fives you. "Great night, guys! See you at the restaurant."

And then he's gone.

"A Whole New World"

PEABO BRYSON AND REGINA BELLE

Your life continues. You wake up, you make coffee, you work on your dissertation, you teach your class, you read, you make more coffee, you read some more, you wait tables at the restaurant, you make good tips, you go out with some of the waitstaff after your shift. Later, you will look back and marvel that all of this simply went on without any seeming interruption, despite how at a loss you felt. How sad, how awful, how bereft. Even talking with Laura, whom you still call every Thursday evening—even these chats, as pleasant and enjoyable as they are, offer only temporary relief.

You admit to yourself, in your most private moments, you are heartsick. You recognize at least that much. You are heartsick. Even brokenhearted. In time you will know this is not particularly about Ethan—though, Ethan, why, why, why?—but about a string of such catastrophes, a long thread that you keep hoping will wrap itself around you as a life line and pull you back into the safety of a man's arms, a brother's, a father's—hell, even the safety of the son that the counselor says god will grant you, to love you, to heal you.

But it's not to be. Your father won't love you. Neither will Ethan. Glen is already gone. And you can't imagine having a son. You can't imagine having children at all. You don't feel a reproductive imperative. Quite the opposite: you feel an anti-reproductive imperative, a need to cut off this bloodline, to stop these neuroses, these preoccupations, this potential for such bad feeling.

Funny how you've internalized all of this, the pain of your various exclusions and the legacies of bullying. The phone call that promises you'll be in the hospital, so broken your mother can't pay your medical bills. Or worse, dead—dead like faggots deserve. Sacrificed for the greater good, the glory of god, the church, the holy body of Christ. And of course, Christ—the only begotten son, forsaken by his father, sacrificed. That's the only way Christianity can imagine healing, reconciliation, forgiveness. There must be a sacrifice, but not just any old sacrifice—a giving up, a relinquishing, a murdering even of the thing you hold most dear, the thing that is actually part of you . . . cut off, sent away, killed. *Each man kills the thing he loves*, Oscar Wilde writes in exile. But that's not the dictate from just a poisoned queer point of view. It's the formula of love handed down by the divinity itself. You love, you lose. Kill your darling now.

So that is what you do. If this is how it must be, then you will make the sacrifice. You will give up on this desire and pursuit of the whole . . . a whole you, loved at last by a man.

Jasmine never mentions the incident, but even so, at the restaurant, you ignore Ethan. You won't even look at him. You turn away. He doesn't push the point. You're not talking? Okay, he's not talking either. He doesn't ask why. He just accepts. This is, after all, how men are taught to be around one another. No need to talk about emotions, what we feel for each other, discuss our "relationship." If it's not there, it's not there. No need to acknowledge an absence. No need to acknowledge each other at all.

You press on toward finishing your degree, Laura finishes hers, and one evening during the Christmas break, she basically calls the question: "Where is this going? What are we doing here?"

You know what she's asking. So you ask in turn, "Are you saying you want to get married?"

"Do you?" she asks back.

"I guess so."

"Okay, then."

Or something to that effect. You don't exactly propose, and neither does she. What's between you has never been conventional anyway. Why start now? So you decide together: this coming summer, after graduation, you'll start your lives. Together.

Married.

You are excited, no doubt. This has seemed inevitable. You've given up on your other dreams, one in particular that has stretched back and back and back, past Ethan and Matt, past Glen and all the way to your adolescence and the bullying, the exclusion—the desire to be held by a man, by your man.

But wait, wait. Is it that easy, really that easy? Just a speech act, a declaration, an "I do" to heterosexuality? In the weeks before your nuptials, you start to worry that something's wrong. You start to remember vividly all of the scenes with Mike, in your bed, your dorm-room bed—the kissing, the cock-sucking, the fingers up the ass. Oh my god. You could be . . . infected. You could have HIV. You could have AIDS. The ALL CAPS serve as a typographical metonym for the SEVERITY of the situation. For the SEVERITY of YOUR situation.

There's only one thing to do. You must get tested. *You must get tested.* And no one can find out about it.

So one late spring afternoon, hot and sticky, in the secondhand sports coat you teach in, you go to the student health center. No questions and documentation needed, no identifying information collected. You sit in the clinic while the nurse draws your blood. Another nurse inquires what test you are getting, and shaking her head with disgust, your bloodletter tells her: "That AIDS test."

You are mortified. You've already sinned and been tried, judged, and now—possibly sentenced.

Two weeks later, you call to find out your test result, and when the nurse on the line pauses and says, "I'll have to let you talk to a doctor," you stop breathing. Even now, writing out this story, your future breath shortens, because in that moment, you think you are about to receive a death sentence.

Then the doctor comes on the phone and tells you that you are negative, everything is fine, that only a doctor (at that time, in that place, deep in Louisiana, in 1993) can report such test results. Standing in your mother's kitchen, you want to, but won't, sob with relief. Only later will you get angry. Why couldn't the nurse tell you that a doctor had to report the result? That abrupt and dismissive response—"I'll have to let you talk to a doctor"—was clearly designed to punish you for seeking out the test, . . . for having done something that caused you to want to take it.

But what do they know? Nothing about you. Nothing, nada, zilch. And just a few weeks later, once more sitting in your parent's kitchen, breaking down, finally, and sobbing—sobbing, because the stress of it all is just too much—whom do you have to talk to about any of this, about *all* of this? No one, no one, no one but that counselor, who has made god promise to give you a son. And your father, sitting across from you, the generally silent one, the distant one, the all-but-dismissive one—he knows. This is not just the normal stress of getting married. There's something wrong here. Something amiss.

"You're a homosexual, aren't you?"

"Well, close, Dad. Close."

You talk about Glen, your story. Your parents want to know what you're going to do.

"I'm getting married this summer."

Neither set of parents is especially thrilled, for their own reasons. Your father likely suspects it cannot last. Your mother, well, perhaps she's jealous that you're leaving her. Laura's parents never warm to you; you're too nerdy, bookish. Their collective resistance emboldens you both all the more. *Fuck them*, both you and Laura think. *We'll show them. Who the fuck are they, telling us what to do? Not like they haven't made messes of their own lives.*

Ah, the unfairnesses of youth, the judgments, the resentments already birthing.

When the day arrives, the ceremony will actually be quite nice. You will even play the piano for one song, accompanying your church's choir. *As for me and my house, we will serve the Lord.* And you will try. After all, he hasn't left you much else, now has he?

"Will You Be There"

MICHAEL JACKSON

Before the wedding, one night, in your apartment in Baton Rouge, after having taught and read and written, perhaps even after one of your marathon masturbation sessions, you're in the shower, alone, hot water streaming around you. You stand still, and as on so many other occasions, the nearly scalding water feels good on your white flesh—good, scouring, cleansing. It's good to be alive, to be clean.

You're thinking back on the day, thinking of what you've written about the poets, always the poets—Whitman expansive and containing multitudes; Rimbaud wanting a poetry that he could taste and smell, imagining the I as an other; and Hopkins, the priest, the lovelorn priest, sacrificing everything for god, writing his dead letters to a divinity that has already made the greatest sacrifice and only asks that you do the same—all of these poets . . .

. . . and you sense, you feel, you can almost see these spirits, these . . . demons, perhaps, flying over the shower stall and into your chest, just pouring in, these ethereal beings, invading you. You stand, hot water cascading around you, arms slightly extended, as you silently receive the multitudes, the legion of spirits, possibly demons . . . silently because there's nothing inside anyway. There is no self.

I is not just an other. You are not anything at all.

1996

"Who Will Save Your Soul"

JEWEL

All things being equal, you have a habit of saying. But what, really, does that mean? You have come to understand—you know in your bones, and at the base of your cock—that things are never equal, no matter what you're talking about, but especially in the area of desire, the desires that still keep you awake at night, that plague you throughout the day, that simultaneously animate and devastate the motions that you go through and call your life. Your desires are never equal to those of others. They never have been, and they likely never will be, no matter what legislation is passed in the future, no matter what tolerances-leaning-toward-picayunish-acceptance might emerge in the coming decades. What you want is just not acceptable. You are other, even deeply in your closet, where you keep your khakis and your plaid shirts, your topsiders and your woven leather belts. Straight drag. And, boy, isn't it—a drag, that is.

Except, of course, when it isn't. All things being equal, the three years of your married life are not that bad, actually not bad at all. Come to think of it, they are pretty good. You like Laura. You love Laura. In your own way, you are even in love with Laura. You're not sexually drawn to her like you are to men, some men, particular kinds of men. Ethan. D. from high school. Matt. But you don't think of these boys. Mostly. They are part of what has been put aside, a life not taken.

It could be said that the whole country has put aside some things: the Reagan years, the Cold War, the imminent threat of nuclear destruction. Bill Clinton pretty much swept into office at the beginning of the decade to the tune of "Don't Stop Believing." So retro. Almost like the country wanted to revive an earlier era, a hippie world of hope, good vibes, positivity, utopian leaning. It didn't last then. You suspect it won't last now, in the middle of the '90s.

You have already given up.

On some things. With regard to other things, life is . . . good. After graduation, you and Laura move to Colorado Springs, where she takes a job as a counselor at a school for the deaf and you quickly find adjunct and then full-time (if non-tenurable) work teaching writing and literature at a state university in Pueblo. The Front Range. Beautiful, of course— and still a little bit of the Wild West. Still a sense of openness, broad expanses, pristine peaks. The frontier. Westward ho! You love how the mountains (to the west of Colorado Springs and Pueblo) change colors over the course of the day, shifting greens and purples and ruddy browns. So different from the muddy swamps and spillways around which you grew up. And the sky, the sky! You can see for miles and miles, cumulus clouds building up into spectacular towers in the distance. Stunning. You and Laura spend time just looking into the distances, wondering.

You also enjoy teaching—performing the role of teacher. You're just a little bit older (less than a decade!) than your students, but oh, what a gulf of time that is. You show them that, a little farther down the road, on the other side of graduation, a world opens up, a whole new set of possibilities.

Adulthood, yes, is serious business; you two are basically living paycheck to paycheck. But it's okay. Movies, dinners, books, and even the occasional act of making love.

And for you, it *is* an act of love, though you are not at all averse to vaginal intercourse. Later you will express concern for those gay men you come to know who find it "disgusting." You actually enjoy the feel of her vagina closing around your cock. Even when her period catches you both by surprise on one occasion, and you pull out of her, bloodied, you're not repulsed. It doesn't matter. You do love her.

But you don't dream of her at night. And while you think of her throughout the day and look forward to seeing her each evening, cooking together, watching another Hitchcock movie (you're on a Hitchcock kick; such fun to watch these old movies), you also think of the cute student in your class—a big boy, black hair, a bit goofy. Yes, sure, there's the warm feeling of home with Laura at night, after teaching and grading papers and gossiping with colleagues; but then there's the charge, the thrill, even the jolt of seeing this young man as you walk into your class, as he appears in the doorway of your office, as he starts to confide in you some of his concerns—first about his performance in the course, then about the direction of his life—and you catch yourself thinking both *Yes, yes, I can help you*, and *No, no, you need to stay away*. But isn't it all right? *Isn't it?* You're his teacher, for godsakes. You are supposed to help him. Listen to him. Guide him. And if your eye skates down once or twice as you consider his words, his rambling about his late-adolescent, early-adult confusion, consternation, and bewilderment—if your eye drops to his crotch . . .

It will always be like this, won't it? It will never change. All that old misery, back again. Temptations returning.

You begin to think you won't survive this. You have considered suicide in the past, alone in a tub, in the dark hours of night, realizing Ethan won't love you, at least not the way you want him to. But this is all so cliché, isn't it? Stereotypical? A tad . . . overwrought? Is it really all that bad?

And the answer is *Yes, yes it is*. That said, you likely won't die if you remain married. It's not the end of the world. Well, the end of some worlds, and even though you remind yourself you've already forsaken them, you haven't. Not really. No, they are still there. When teaching, you know your step is a little lighter as you walk over to assist a young man. And though it's not remotely fair to your female students, you show more interest when conferencing with male students. You ask questions. You know you do. *What's your major?* You will blush at the memory. Not that you intend to do anything. But you're engaged, you're inquiring, you're pushing—at what? Whatever it is can remain suspended between you and the young man in your office. It need never go any further than the casual interest of a teacher in a promising student.

But it does go further, through the calculus of displacement. You pick up your work again—the completed dissertation on Whitman, Rimbaud, Hopkins—and you think, *Hmmm, what next?* You're invited to give a pre-performance talk on a student staging of *The Importance of Being Earnest*, and you agree, as a scholar of nineteenth-century literature, even though you don't know much about Wilde. But you find out. You read, extensively. And then further. You become obsessed. The plays, *Earnest* and then *A Woman of No Importance*, and then all of them. And the stories, the fairy tales, the serialized novel *The Picture of Dorian Gray*, the art criticism, the dialogues as essays, "The Decay of Lying." Then biographies and the critical literature. So much, so fucking much about this figure who didn't produce a large oeuvre but whose life was his art—and what a life, what a work of art! Reams and reams of paper have been sacrificed to analyze the writings of this one sad, pathetic man, whose spectacular fall from grace created a narrative more powerful than most of what he wrote.

The trial, the trial of the century, helping to bring the Victorian era to a close while ruining a man's life—a man who tried to stand up, then faltered, who was the toast of a town bent on punishing the artist, the critic, who goes a little too far. The record reveals a shaky story, with Wilde decrying any wrongdoing despite the evidence stacked again him ("gross indecency" with a variety of working boys, not just Bosie, dear Bosie), while also feebly challenging the London court not to condemn him for the purity of his love—such a love as an older man might have for a younger man, a love dating back to the very foundations of our civilization in ancient Greek culture. . . .

But they weren't buying it. You don't blame them. He not only transgressed, he flaunted. He threw it in their faces at times. Doesn't one of the male aesthetes in *The Importance of Being Earnest* refer to going to the country to have some fun by saying he's going to visit his dear sick friend, Bunbury? He's going bunburying—as in burying something in "buns." The crowds laughed until they didn't. They toasted the author until they roasted him alive.

It's all there, the rise and downfall, presaged by *The Picture of Dorian Gray*, such a morality tale, the eternally youthful man, so charming, so toxic to his friends, not to mention the naive actress who falls in love with him—this young man, sinning, sinning, never getting older, and then doomed, doomed to discovery, his secret in the upstairs closet coming out to destroy his life.

You pick up your pen to start a critical essay, to write about Wilde, and you realize you're deflecting again. Aren't you? You know what's up. You're obsessed with this story. Laura sees it. She asks, point blank, "Why are so many of the authors you're interested in gay?" As though you made them gay by your interest? But you know what she's really asking. And you have to ask yourself the same question.

What are you doing here?

"Til I Hear It From You"

GIN BLOSSOMS

The question becomes more pressing when you are asked to give a lecture in March, in celebration of Women's History Month.

You've gotten to know some of the folks at the college, particularly a professor of psychology, Karen, who will become a lifelong friend. You don't know that yet, but she will . . . and at the time you hope she will. She caught you photocopying a story about Brandon Teena, the young person with a vagina who was presenting as a man, and who, when "discovered," was brutally beaten, raped, and killed. A cautionary tale? You're teaching it in your writing class—the story, that is; the complexity of documenting, writing about, and arguing through a difficult situation. Karen studies the psychology of gender and sexuality, with a specialty in sexual violence, so she's interested in Brandon Teena. She strikes up a conversation. Unlike most people in your life, she's the one approaching; she's initiating. You don't have to. She's interested in *you*.

At coffee and lunch dates, you exchange stories of teaching, talk about your lives, get to know one another better. You learn Karen's in a relationship with a young woman. Your eyebrow raises. You're married, you tell her. "To a woman," you add, before rushing to say, in an effort to impress her, "but I have, you know, had experiences." She doesn't bat an eye. You don't desire her, and you don't think she desires you either.

Not bodily. But you love that she reached out. She loves that you reached back. You both love that you can confide in one another.

"I thought you might be family," she says, smiling a little.

You smile back.

Fuck me, this feels good, you think. And it does.

Family.

That night, at home, you talk about your new friend. Laura frowns, then the expression smooths as she realizes that Karen isn't a threat. Not exactly. But you're only guessing what she's thinking.

In time, all four of you have some lovely double dates out, laughing, enjoying one another's company. It's good. Life is good. *Family.*

Knowing of your interest in Whitman, Wilde, and others, Karen asks if you'll participate in Women's History Month, giving a lecture on a topic of your choice . . . anything . . . perhaps something about a queer author? You succumb to the pressure because, well, you're junior faculty, *really* junior faculty, and it's good to show that you're involved, that you're participating, that you're a team player.

But no, more than that. You want to talk about . . . something. You want to talk about what it's like teaching all these young people, these beautiful young people, these young souls who look up to you, who trust you, who want guidance, who need you. And how you want their interest, their desire . . . to learn from you. Yes, you want to talk about the young man sitting in your office, not how you're checking out his crotch, but how he is drawn to you and you are drawn to him and the circle reinforces how you both need each other and learn from each other and (hopefully) grow together. While writing out these thoughts, you realize that you have a unique way to conceptualize them (or at least what you think will be a catchy title), something provocative but also (hopefully) evocative before the de rigueur colon and the academic jargon: Bisexual Pedagogy: Transference, Counter-Transference, and Student/Teacher Learning.

Future you will blush at the pretentiousness, but in the moment you're in love with it. You even ask a friend to make some original art for the poster, and she does, a lovely image of three figures, in three colors (pink, yellow, and blue), overlapping one another. You photocopy the poster at Kinko's for distribution around campus.

You are thrilled at having turned part of your tortured longing, your forsaken desire, into something good, into an academic treatise, a statement. And the event itself, the event is amazing. Your paper is well received, colleagues nodding in agreement. You're feeling good, really good. And then, in the Q&A, you open up even more and talk about how your own bisexual experiences in college helped you be more receptive to both male and female students. But wait . . .

"I'm bisexual."

The moment almost passes without you noticing. And then, you notice. You notice there's no gasp from the audience, no horror. Just smiles. Who knows what people are thinking, but no one is throwing a stone. Not yet. And there's even the cute guy who comes up to you after your talk, a student asking questions, wanting to know more about your thoughts on teaching, wondering which of your classes he might take. He's a psychology minor, clearly interested in your style. As you continue to chat, you realize he's . . . flirting. You blush, put him off a little, freeze up because you are unused to this—but you're deeply flattered. Even moved. (Spoiler alert: you'll eventually marry this man.)

And Laura, dear Laura. She too is in the audience, smiling, supportive. She knows some of your past, your struggles. She has heard you name them. She has seen you recuperate from them, or at least try to. You are grateful to her for being there, for supporting you. For understanding. You are moved by your love, her love.

At the same time, however, you can hear Oscar Wilde whispering in your ear. It's a faint tickle, like a mosquito getting too close, something you bat with your hand, automatically swatting. But still there, buzzing back. You can't help but lean in to the sound, a voice, saying something, murmuring even as you swat, swat, swat. . . .

Each man kills the thing he loves. The phrase comes to you, from *The Importance of Being Earnest*. A bit of queer wisdom cutting through the swarm of discourse surrounding you far away in Colorado, away from your Louisiana roots, the wild swamps of homophobia. Yes, don't forget that Wilde's life is a cautionary tale. Attend to what happened to him, his degradation and downfall. Your upbringing in the Deep South, your Catholic education, your rejection by the men you wanted to love you, love you in terrible, terrible ways—these are the twitches on the thread that have pulled you back from the brink. Wilde's life is speaking to you from across the decades. *Each man kills the thing he loves.*

And then, for once, quietly, you begin to hear this sentence differently. Of course, of course, you've been hearing it as the problem of desire, the propulsion behind our cravings that kills us when we give in to them. That's the example of Dorian Gray. Some desires are dangerous—deadly, even, because they are wrong. Illegal. But take also "The Ballad of Reading Gaol," the long poem Wilde wrote in exile, in the scant three years between being released from prison and his impoverished death. The lines speak of this destructiveness of desire, yes, but they also speak of the destruction we ourselves face when desire turns back on itself: we destroy what we love, perhaps, because we don't believe we deserve to have it.

You ask yourself, what have you been loving? And what have you kept yourself from loving? And what might happen if you kill the thing you do love, so you can start loving something else?

The phone rings later that week. It's Laura, calling from her night job at a suicide-prevention hotline. She usually checks in once she gets to work, not long before you head to bed.

She's crying. "I think we should get a divorce."

You're silent for a half minute. "Okay. Yeah."

In this way, she teaches you the first lesson in killing the thing you love: your connection to each other. You both need to move on, to continue your searches for what you really want. You've helped each other so far by linking together; now you help yourselves by letting go.

You will always be grateful—for the help, for the love, and for the letting go.

"Closer to Free"

THE BODEANS

After you get off the phone, you feel like a loser. You will be divorced. Losers get divorced. A few tears roll down. The pity party lasts for about a half hour. And then, strangely, you laugh at yourself. You're starting to move on, at least emotionally. You still need to divide your belongings, move out of the house, but already you're thinking you'll find a place closer to campus, cut down on your commute. Already you're thinking about expenses, how to save money, what additional income you might try to bring in. In the coming weeks, you keep yourself busy. You've learned the value of distraction.

Ultimately, though, despite these distractions and your constant planning, some things penetrate. You realize you're not in Louisiana. You've said the word *bisexual* in public, and no one threw a stone. You're not going to be married anymore. The spirit of Wilde might be whispering in your ear, but he's long dead, god rest his tortured soul.

You—you're not dead yet. Of course, there will always be something standing in your way. There will always be a reason to turn from your desires, to keep them locked in your bedroom, squirming against the bonds with which you restrain them, restrain yourself—alone, alone, more lonely than not.

Yes, there will always be impediments. But you find there are opportunities too.

Newly gay, er bisexual, you have a vested interest, suddenly, in Colorado's Amendment 2, which passed shortly before you moved to the state and sparked a series of appeals that now, in 1996, had wound their way up to the US Supreme Court.

Amendment 2 was initially spurred on by antigay groups to stem the tide of LGBT-affirming laws and legislation that had been on the rise all over the country since at least the '70s. While some jurisdictions steadily voted to extend various civil protections to queers, others tried to block such protections. Amendment 2's authors were in the latter camp, the descendants of Anita Bryant, dear Anita, whose 1977 Save Our Children campaign aimed to overturn a Florida county's ordinance that prohibited discrimination on the basis of sexual orientation. Bryant was successful, and she literally danced when a majority of voters repealed the ordinance, asserting, "All America and all the world will hear what the people have said, and with God's continued help, we will prevail in our fight to repeal similar laws throughout the nation which attempt to legitimize a lifestyle that is both perverse and dangerous."

Fifteen years later, Amendment 2 followed suit, attempting to make it impossible for Colorado to extend protections to queers. To wit, the law stated,

> Neither the State of Colorado, through any of its branches or departments, nor any of its agencies, political subdivisions, municipalities or school districts, shall enact, adopt or enforce any statute, regulation, ordinance or policy whereby homosexual, lesbian or bisexual orientation, conduct, practices or relationships shall constitute or otherwise be the basis of or entitle any person or class of persons to have or claim any minority status, quota preferences, protected status or claim of discrimination. This Section of the Constitution shall be in all respects self-executing.

Karen sends you a copy of this text, wanting to talk about it, wanting to get your thoughts because the news cycle is heating up, journalists are writing about this, the Supreme Court is going to weigh in. More than weigh in: they are going to decide, finally and for all, if this kind of law is "Constitutional." And then the realization hits.

This is a law about you.

It's like a slap in the face, a fist in the gut, a sucker punch. You've just stepped out of the closet into the shit-smeared outhouse of second-class citizenship. You're fucked, long before you have even been properly fucked. You could be kicked out of your new post-divorce apartment. It's all you can afford, these squalid two rooms with no furniture on the south side of town, the icky side, and yet the landlord can say, "I want you out because you're a faggot, a dirty little cocksucking, fudge-packing faggot"—and there's nothing you can do about it. You'd have no legal recourse. Nada, zip, zilch.

This is a law about you.

And after all this time, even after your failed marriage, your divorce, you think, *No. Not acceptable. I'm not a loser.* There will always be an impediment. But maybe, maybe, you won't be your own impediment anymore.

"The World I Know"

COLLECTIVE SOUL

Karen, the only openly queer person on your campus, is a little surprised by how emboldened you suddenly feel. Recently divorced, publicly declaring yourself bisexual, you immediately propose teaching courses on queer literature, a special honors seminar on Oscar Wilde; you host an LGBT poetry reading; you become the faculty sponsor of the LGBT student organization. You have, as one of Karen's lesbian friends puts it, just "busted" out of the closet. It's what men do, apparently. When they come out, they explode out.

Too long, you think. You had to wait too long.

Then again, that's not entirely true. There are many ways to tell this story, aren't there?

You might say, for instance, that you held yourself back, except when you didn't. You had a possible trauma with an uncle, an affair with Mike, the drama of the Film Committee. You had all your tortured feelings for various guys. You've spent so much of your life trying to desire differently—first wanting to *not* desire, desperately wishing you weren't the faggot you strongly suspected you might be; then wanting to desire what you'd been told to desire; and now wanting to desire something you'd been taught was unacceptable, to embrace the queernesses within, to fly in the face of the heteropatriarchy that had been keeping you in check.

Back and forth. You've tried so many ways to deal with your desires, your queerness. Even the story you told about Glen, whatever happened with Glen, was a way to talk about what you wanted, how you wanted to love, whom you wanted to love. And whom you wanted to love you back.

You've tried to be honest, as honest as you could be within the limits of church and state, culture and politics, family and friends. You haven't always hidden. Your closet has been a porous thing, and while you may now be busting out, you can't bring yourself to renounce what came before. Not quite. Maybe not ever. This is not a before and an after. This is not "was straight" and "now gay." You've never felt straight, even if you haven't always felt gay.

Truth be told, you won't always feel gay from this point forward.

Years from now, you'll sit with a group of gay guys in a restaurant in the Midwest and talk about your "past lives," so many gay lives being divided into *before* and *after*, a closet self and then an out, "true" self. You will talk about having been married, and inevitably the question will come: didn't you know? Yes, in a way, and no, you'll say. You loved her. You were even what you would call "in love."

"Eww. The sex . . . with a vagina."

"Well, I actually liked it."

"What!? Bullshit. No gay man wants fish for sex. What kind of fag are you?"

Don't worry. You won't spend much time with these gay men. No shade on them, except for their sexism. They are not your tribe; you will find more compatible queers elsewhere.

In 1996, though, in your two-room apartment, a thin futon for your bed, a milk crate to support a reading lamp, you sit on the toilet, having just fetched the mail after getting home from work. You sift through the junk, junk, bill, bill, junk . . . and then, what's this? Something from the State of Colorado? You open it up, and it's the court-signed divorce decree. The claim of irreconcilable differences has been accepted by the state. You are officially divorced.

You remember—you will likely always remember—going to the

courthouse with Laura, with all the other divorcing couples, for an information session on what you had to do to file. A somber occasion for many, practically everyone, there. But you two are making jokes, cutting up. You absolutely understand the seriousness of what you're doing. Your marriage was not a lark. Splitting up has been no laughing matter. (But hey, some of it is funny: the formality, the bailiff, the reverential tone of the whole proceeding. It's just an information session. Why so serious?) But you know, and Laura knows, that the greatest act of love you can offer each other is freedom—freedom while you're both still young, without the encumbrances of property or children, the freedom to go off and fuck . . . uh, do whatever, with whomever you want to do it with.

Then again, you think as you sit on your toilet, the decree in hand: is this the greatest act of love? You were not the one asking for the divorce, though you in no way fault Laura for doing so. In truth—and it's a truth those gay boys in the Midwest would likely never understand— you could've stayed married. You would've stayed married. You didn't necessarily want a divorce. Certainly, something would've had to give, some accommodation needed to be made, by and for both of you. But you would have been willing to go for it, give something different a try, experiment broadly with your life—and hers, if she'd been game.

At least, you thought you would have been willing. You still do, as happy as you are now, "gay married" to a man. You wonder: what would your life have been like if you and Laura had stayed together, had opened up your relationship, had just done things differently? Sitting on that toilet in 1996, you have no regrets (and you will have none in the future), at least not about the divorce. But you do wonder.

So you are back to your earlier proposition, your emerging way of thinking about your life—how you have spent much of it trying to desire differently. *Spent*—the word gives you pause. To characterize time, life, as some kind of financial transaction, leaving one with less . . .

No, you want a different formulation, another way of thinking about where you find yourself now, on the john in a shabby apartment on the south side of town, holding a divorce decree, newly "out," and not really knowing what to do. The only question that seems right, the only one that comes to you, is, at first, a strange question: *what does it mean to desire differently?*

Then another surfaces: *can I be other than what I am?*

You're about to find out.

"If It Makes You Happy"

SHERYL CROW

Maybe what you are feeling, for once, is how you are entering history. Of course, you are never not already in it. But when have you hâd the chance to feel history, and feel yourself, your life, as part of history?

Perhaps you are just getting older. Don't worry: you are young yet, oh so very young. You have more than enough time to consider the question, which will come to you as surely as your first gray hair: *what remains of all that misery, all the history of misery?* Your trick, something you'll accept as a gift, will be to note how misery is never entirely yours alone, to understand that something, perhaps what people call "history," surrounds you, us, and all of us are swayed by it, that it ripples constantly under and around and through us, moves us gently up and down and from side to side, and then, at times, not so gently, but suddenly, roughly, even catastrophically.

Your catastrophe still awaits you, even though you feel (write it!) like you're already going through it. But no, not yet.

What you are going through, at this point in the chronology, is the possibility of having a real live gay date. That's right, and that's how you're thinking of it. In your mind, the collegiate, senior-year interlude with Mike doesn't quite count as your "gay time." Sure, you were dating a boy, and you were basically "out" to the Film Committee, but so much of that doesn't come down to you as real. Not really gay. More like playing at being gay. But now, on the other side of your divorce, on the other side of having given heterosexuality a good adult try, on the other side of publicly labelling yourself a "bisexual," you feel there's no safety net. Maybe being "out" is a dividing line, after all. (You'll go back and forth on this for a while.)

As your older self writes this, he is mindful that you have not yet told your parents. Yes, you have told them about the divorce. Mother doesn't quite say she's surprised the marriage lasted as long as it did, but there's relief in her response to the news, as in, *Thank god that's over.* She will not ask what's coming next. Though you don't think she wants you to be lonely, she seems most comfortable imagining you alone. She just doesn't like to think of you with a mate. You're not sure why. But you grasp it's best to refrain from mentioning that your divorce coincides with your decision to "come out," to start pursuing a decidedly "gay lifestyle." She would not approve, even as your father, you instinctively know, would not be especially surprised—and would almost surely not care. But your mother would. In fact, when you've been divorced a couple of years and have found the person you'll likely spend the rest of your days with, you will call her up to talk about him, the man you are dating, and she will interrupt you, pointedly, and say, "I don't want to hear about the evil in your life." You won't be able to respond immediately, and in the silence she will finish her thought with words no child wants to hear, whatever the circumstances, whatever the historical and personal particulars: "We don't love you for who you are. We love you for the person we know you could be."

In that moment, you will choose to commit all the more to the life you have chosen—not out of any spite or resentment, but because you will be free, finally and fully free, from any sense that you are beholden to your parents; if they can relinquish the parental prerogative to love unconditionally, then you can relinquish any sense of responsibility to them. This wound—and wound it is, despite the stoicism with which you receive it—will eventually heal. Things will change. Your relationship to both your father and your mother will alter. But that is the subject of a different book. For now, for the you that lies between your just-divorced self and the future self writing these words, there is much yet to experience, much yet to try to understand.

You meet Shawn through Karen. A graduate of the university where you teach, he is her former student, an English major, of all things, and someone still involved in the student lesbian and gay group of which you're faculty sponsor. He lives in Pueblo and shows up at meetings sometimes, saying hello, offering his thoughts, an older brother's shoulder. You take note because, well, he's cute. And not a student. That's important. You don't want to be the professor who fucks his students. That's such a hetero cliché. No need to tempt people to think it's also a gay cliché.

Ah, the things you need to think about now that you're queer.

And indeed, you have some gaps in your knowledge base. It's been a while since you've been on a date, since you've asked someone out. You don't know if Shawn's remotely interested in you. He seems friendly enough, and once you thought you saw him looking at you before quickly turning away. *Oh, fuck,* you think, *so many guessing games. Why can't we all just wear cards that announce what we're looking for?*

Curiously, you soon realize there is a place where people wear just such identifying cards. It's called the Internet, and since your divorce, you've stuck around the computer lab you teach writing in, waiting until everyone is gone and the room is officially closed so you can, as you say, "catch up on some work," but really, once the light in the outer hall goes off, you start cruising websites for porn. Gay porn. Raunchy, nasty, cocksucking, ass-fucking porn. You find a whole ever-expanding world of guys fucking, fisting, tying each other up, and spanking one another. It's incredible. There's even a site built around a play prison, with what look like real jail cells, in which men imprison one another, taking turns in bondage gear, teasing and torturing one another, fucking. You've hit the jackpot. Even if you don't know how to do any of this stuff in real life, you can still enjoy it on the screen. You can learn. You see a boy spread-eagled on a bed, facedown, the pixelated image slowly resolving—it is 1996, after all—your right hand clicking on the mouse to download other images in the sequence, such as the bearish top with a paddle poised over the now gagged boy, and with your left hand you reach down to your crotch. . . .

A sudden jangle at the door; a key going in.

Fuck.

You quickly click away from the pages. It's Heather, the super-smart poet who works primarily as the school's technology support.

"Hey, didn't know anyone was in here! Just checking on the server."

"No problem! Just finishing up some work."

"Cool, cool."

She disappears into the backroom to do her thing, and you start to pack your bag. But first you clear the cache. You know enough to do that. And you do it every time—much to Heather's chagrin, you will discover, because sometimes she goes searching for images she's seen during her own web surfing . . . But nope. You have learned to cover your tracks. After all, you've been doing a version of clearing the cache for years.

"Be My Lover"

LA BOUCHE

You've seen the message boards and the chat rooms. People actually announce, often pretty baldly, what they want to do. You could find someone online. You could even find someone to date. It's not all just sex, sex, sex, though that idea is titillating. But Shawn is at hand, as they say. He's here. Not an image or descriptive text on a screen, but a real live human being who happens to be gay. You should ask him out, you think.

You don't quite have the nerve.

Then, to celebrate the end of spring term and the beginning of summer, Karen invites you and a little queer group of friends—including Shawn—to a gay dance club (one of the few in the region) in Colorado Springs. Beforehand, you and Karen have dinner. She's encouraging. She knows you'd like to ask Shawn on a date but you're not sure how, or if he'd even be open to the possibility.

"Uh, that's why you have to ask."

"Yeah, I guess you're right."

The club is dark and smoky, also loud, so it's hard for people to talk, which you suppose is okay since that forestalls (1) you asking Shawn on a date or (2) you chickening out—both stomach-churning potentialities. You get a screwdriver. Liquid courage, they call it, but also numbing, the vodka burning but promising, too, that you don't have to think about what you don't want to think about, not for a while.

But no, no, NO; you will think about it. You agreed to get divorced, for fuck's sake, so you could have this moment. Deafening music or not, you are going to do this.

Steeling yourself, you head to the dance floor where Shawn and his friends are already spinning and gyrating or, as the case may be, swaying stiltedly side to side. Shawn, bless him, is more a swayer than a gyrater. You're charmed. You move closer and, shit, he seems to turn away. But wait, that was just a more adventuresome sway. You lean in again, say hello.

"Hey," he responds with a nod and, maybe, is that a smile? Could be a smirk. Is he signaling that he's not interested? *What the fuck.*

You bend in. "Hey, I was wondering, would you like to get a coffee sometime soon?" You don't think you're breathing. But you are, and . . . so is he, as his mouth curves upward.

"Yeah," he says, then looks away, still smiling. "I'd like that."

"Okay, cool. Okay." You start laughing, and so does he.

Karen's ready to head home, and she's your ride, so you are saved from further awkward conversation. You leave the club earlier than the rest of the group, but you got what you came for. A sign. A way forward. A path opening.

"Give Me One Reason" or "Nobody Knows"

TRACY CHAPMAN / THE TONY RICH PROJECT

The next day you're on a plane for a visit with your parents and sisters. You don't really want to go, but then again you do. *It's complicated*, as they will come to say. Your new life beckons, and your parents are part of the old. While they know you're divorced, they are fuzzy on the details, and you're not ready to lift the fuzz. Then again, you've experienced what amounts to a small trauma—a divorce, a coming out—so maybe it's not so bad that you'll be among people you know, seeing familiar faces, even if they're faces that would frown at the full extent of your subjugation by the forces of evil, your turn to the homosexual within.

No, not the time for further revelation. You can save that particular bomb for later.

You have a few quiet days at your parents', enjoying the heat of May in Louisiana, with some rain in the afternoons, which doesn't cool anything off. But still, this sweat feels like home, even if it's one you're leaving more and more. Your mother wants to know what caused the rift between you and Laura. You remain vague. She doesn't push. You consider renting a car and driving to Baton Rouge, perhaps looking up Patty, maybe another long-lost friend or two, but upon further thought, you decide against spending the money. You don't have the collective income of a couple anymore, so best get used to living on less. You do splurge on beignets at the local Morning Call, and order their café au lait (the only time you drink cream in your coffee). It's just too good. And of course you hit a bookstore or two. There's a new big Barnes and Noble to check out right on Veterans, that lengthy commercial strip running through northern Metairie. Yes, there are some comforts of "home." After everything that's been happening, you relax, a little, into the familiarity of it all.

Three, four nights into the trip, just a couple of days left, with your sisters out of the house, on their own, and your mother and father watching television, headed to bed shortly, you find yourself bored, antsy, itching for something to do. Not Baton Rouge . . . but what? A splinter in your mind, one you didn't even know was there, now becomes a throbbing insistence.

Ethan.

You still have his number, his parents' number. You don't know if he's still living with them, but you call and the phone rings and someone, a woman, picks up. *No, he's at work. Okay, thank you.* You hang up, not wanting to leave your name. Your tentativeness surprises you. You've been so much bolder recently. But Ethan is part of the complex past, and you haven't quite figured out yet how to live with that past, much less make peace with it, tell its story in a way you can carry into the future.

Enough navel-gazing; too much reflection. You grab your mother's car keys, tell your parents you're headed to dinner, and you're out the door before they can react. You don't want anything or anyone to derail you now that you're in motion. Last you remember, Ethan was working at the Copeland's uptown. Copeland's, the higher-end restaurant owned by the man, Al Copeland, who invented Popeye's Louisiana Kitchen. The food is actually okay, an attempt to replicate tasty New Orleanian cuisine: fried catfish, crawfish étouffée, seafood gumbo. And steak, of course. It's not cheap, but you're fine splurging one of your last nights in town. Besides, you're already in motion.

You snake up Claiborne and Carrollton to St. Charles, the tree-shaded boulevard with the streetcar tracks separating the two lanes. Go far enough on St. Charles and you get to downtown, but before then, you're solidly uptown, passing Tulane and Loyola, City Park and the Audubon Zoo. And then, Copeland's. The purplish neon beckons. You park and walk in.

"Just one?"

"Yeah, just one. And, uh, is Ethan on tonight?"

"Hold on, let me see if he's got a table free. Hmmm, yes! Right this way."

You sit, wondering what you're doing here. Glancing around, you don't see him, and struck by a fit of nerves, you duck behind your menu. You don't belong here.

"Good evening, sir. Welcome to Copeland's."

Ethan stands beside the table, opening his order pad, not having made eye contact yet. Then he looks up, blue eyes under his tight blond curls.

"Oh. My. God. What the fuck, dude! I haven't seen you in ages!" He leans in, and you think he wants to hug you, but he's at work, so he settles for a clap on the shoulder, his hand lingering on your upper arm.

"Hey, Ethan. What's new?"

You exchange pleasantries and news. He's working here most nights, saving up, unsure of what's next. You're just visiting from Colorado. Yes, Laura's fine, but you're now divorced. No shit!? Yeah, shit, but it's really okay, you assure him. Totally amicable. No bloodletting. All good.

He doesn't have a lot of time to chat but seems happy to exchange more words when he brings you your crawfish étouffée, which you love, even though it always tastes a little . . . dirty.

He drops off the check, with a discount, and surprises you.

"Hey, what are you doing? I'm actually starting my sidework and plan to get out of here in an hour, tops. Come have a drink?"

Of course you will. There's a little dive bar right around the corner. You agree to meet him there.

An hour later, he shows up, still in his black pants and white shirt, his apron left in his car. He orders beer to join your screwdriver and taps his brown bottle against your plastic cup. It's a bit loud to talk, but you try, catching up on the folks from the restaurant—who's doing what now, and with whom. *Shit, I had no idea they were together. Or that they had split up. What whores!* You realize you're part of this ongoing narrative, your life someone else's gossip. But you don't mind.

As Ethan talks at you, enjoying his monologue, you waffle over telling him you're gay or bisexual now. You decide not to. This isn't going anywhere. He's still hot, absolutely, but this is just bullshit, just as much bullshit as what's coming out of his mouth and, to be fair, out of yours. You won't stay in touch. A friendship won't flourish. And you certainly won't be getting into his pants. Hell, you don't even mention the stretch when you two were ignoring each other. There's not enough depth here to have that kind of conversation.

You tell him how nice it's been to see him, that you need to get home. Long day. No worries, man. All good. You leave.

And you never see him again.

At home, about midnight, your parents soundly asleep, you turn on the television and catch a news program—a deeper dive into the day's events than the cataloguing of atrocities that airs at 10. At first the talking heads are just background noise as you take off your jeans, but then you catch a phrase or two—Colorado . . . gay rights—and you pay attention. Then you're practically shitting yourself.

The US Supreme Court has voted, 6 to 3, to overturn Colorado's Amendment 2.

You don't breathe for maybe half a minute, standing in front of the tv in your underpants. Except for low voices of the program, the house is quiet. Then you start to hear a thumping, over and over. It's your heart. You can hear your heartbeat over the intellectual susurrations of the discussion. Thump, thump. Thump, thump. Steady, strong. Your body starts to rock in time with it.

One of the commentators reads from the ruling authored by Anthony Kennedy:

It is a fair, if not necessary, inference from the broad language of the amendment that it deprives gays and lesbians even of the protection of general laws and policies that prohibit arbitrary discrimination in governmental and private settings.

[The Amendment] identifies persons by a single trait and then denies them protection across the board. The resulting disqualification of a class of persons from the right to seek specific protection from the law is unprecedented in our jurisprudence.

Such a reasonable position. Part of you can't believe that the Court came to this simple conclusion: don't discriminate. Don't bar a group of people from the protections of the law. Even in this emotional moment you have the wherewithal to be incredulous that three other members of the Court didn't see anything wrong with making discrimination legal. Then again, you remember *Bowers v. Hardwick*, from 1986, which upheld Georgia's anti-sodomy laws, in effect criminalizing gay sex (and pretty much any nonreproductive sexual act). Such statutes are still the law of the land in many places. You will have to wait until the summer of 2003, and *Lawrence v. Texas*, for one to be overturned federally. For now, though, this decision seems, well, not exactly enough, but a good step. Something positive. A victory, even.

You dig in your bag and pull out Shawn's number. You don't think. You dial. He picks up, a little groggy, but he's only an hour behind. If he's already in bed, he hasn't been there long.

"Did you hear the news?"

"Yes! I can't believe it, man. I really can't believe it."

"It's incredible."

"I know, right!?"

"So, that date I mentioned. What are you doing next Saturday?"

"Because You Loved Me" or
"I Want to Come Over"

CÉLINE DION / MELISSA ETHERIDGE

Your first date with Shawn is surprising only in how "normal" it feels and likely looks, if anyone cared to notice that you're on a date with another man. You pick him up at the house he shares with a few other folks in their mid-twenties—a large, ramshackle green Victorian on a corner not far from downtown (such as downtown is in Pueblo, a municipality of 100,000). He gets in, a bit shy at first. Cute, though, in his shyness. Cute in other ways too. He's a Black man with strong features, also balding a little, something he's self-conscious about, though you don't really notice it; he's just so present, so *with you*, so interested in going on this date. A receding hairline can't detract from that.

You head to one of your favorite local Italian restaurants and order pizza, deliciously greasy and thin crust. You talk about your lives, about your work—he's a teller at a bank— about what you both hope for, what you want out of life, what you fear life is too stingy to offer. But neither of you is ungrateful. You're both healthy, still young, and you have enough to eat. Many are worse off. And with the recent overturning of Amendment 2, things are looking better. You also know how far you've come, how long the road has been to this moment. You wipe pizza grease off your chin. Then you extend your napkin to wipe it off his chin. You don't mind being cliché. Not one bit. Not right now.

Later, alone at home, on your slim futon, you go over the evening. Just in your white briefs, the air still heavy with the heat of the day but quickly cooling in the dryness of the prairie, you refrain from touching yourself. This isn't about sex. Not yet, at least. It will be about that, definitely, but right now you are caught up in thinking this is the happiest moment of the past half million, and you don't want anything like a post-cum melancholy to dim the glow.

And what, really, has happened? Something so simple, yet so difficult. You remember the club in Colorado Springs, the dancing that was more swaying than anything else. You asked someone to look at you, and after a few moments, he did. You asked someone, "Let me in." And he did.

"Change the World"

ERIC CLAPTON

The summer proceeds. You're not teaching any courses, which is probably a shame because you could use the extra money, but you decided to give yourself a break, having just divorced, moved, come out of the closet. Every other day or so, you and Shawn hang out, making dinner, going to the movies—and having sex. Mostly oral and making out. You don't think you're quite ready for the "big stuff," and Shawn isn't pushing. You do swat his butt every once in a while, just a playful slap. He likes it. He smiles shyly. You wonder: is striking, even playfully, the buttocks of a Black man potentially racist? You don't think so. You like asses. You like swatting them, even having yours swatted. You decide to play it by ear, see what happens. See where all of this is going. You don't know yet, but that's okay. You've never felt more . . . present? Is that the cliché you're looking for? You suppose it is.

Present.

Then it's June, late June, and you and Shawn drive to Colorado Springs, just forty minutes to the north, for their Pride celebration, bigger than the one in Pueblo, Springs being about four times the size of the Steel City. It's a bright, warm day. Exhilarating, maybe because Colorado Springs is higher in altitude than Pueblo, the air a tad thinner. But also because it's your first Pride Day. A Sunday. You can't wait.

You get there early, find a place to park on the outskirts of downtown, where there are no parking meters to worry about. You bum around, get a coffee at a hipstery joint where Colorado college kids panhandle for change, pretending they're poor or homeless. You ignore them as you walk with Shawn, looking around as you reach out to hold his hand.

"Hey, not just yet. Let's wait till we get to the park."

He's right. No need to push all of the buttons at the same time. This is, after all, the home, not just of large military installations such as NORAD, but also of Focus on the Family. The home of James Dobson, the worthless motherfucker, homophobic asshole, fascist dick. You're surprised at how venomous your language can be, how righteously indignant you can feel. Where does all that rage come from? You know it's not simply your awakening to the political situation of queer people. It's also from your personal experience, from your own encounters with homophobia, long before you took on the identity of "gay" or "queer" or "bisexual" or "fudge-packing faggot." And maybe some of the anger is aimed at yourself. No, no: you don't blame yourself for not coming out earlier. You have always lived by the truth you've known at the time. You'll hold on to that belief, and even when your relationship to it changes, you will always adhere to a version of it. So no, you're not angry about a relatively belated coming out. There's still time to enjoy yourself, your young self, and the young selves of others. But you *are* angry at yourself for taking all the shit said about you, thrown at you. You think of monkeys in a cage, playing with their shit, caged, bored, trapped, flinging it at each other, at the visitors to the zoo. Even when it was coming at you, you kept your shit to yourself. You wish you'd thrown some back.

You think you'll start throwing some now.

But first, the Pride Parade—the marchers, the various activist groups, few in number but fierce in commitment, and the small businesses that want all of that supposed gay money, which you certainly don't have, but you're still happy to see them showing their support the only way they know how, which is something. And then, then, an older crew, this time from PFLAG—Parents and Friends of Lesbians and Gays—mothers and fathers and sisters and brothers and other assorted folk, mostly straight allies. You and Shawn fall silent, his hand finally reaching for yours. A tear comes to your eye, and to Shawn's. Neither of you has to say anything, nothing at all.

You both make your way to the vendors selling t-shirts and trinkets, moving from stall to stall, checking out the rainbow-bedecked t-shirts and necklaces. Suddenly a television reporter stops you and Shawn, with camera crew in tow. You're already sporting "rings," a necklace holding a set of small metal rings in the day's festive ROYGBIV colors. Shawn is looking stylish in a tight-fitting black t-shirt. Of course—a Black man, a white man, both obviously gay—you're approached for comment about this momentous day, the first celebration after the Supreme Court's decision to overturn this state's discriminatory ordinance.

You don't even think about saying no. You offer a statement, camera rolling. Later, you won't remember *what* you said, just that you said something, marking the moment, for yourself, for Shawn, for others. You were there. And you know enough about history, about the Stonewall Riots, the uprising of trans folk and drag queens and gay boys and lesbians and other queers who fought back against police constantly raiding their bars, some of the few places they could congregate—never really safely, mind you, given the frequency of raids, or the mobs squeezing the queer bar owners for every penny they could—no, you know enough to understand that this Pride celebration, which commemorates the Stonewall Riots, is nowhere near as dangerous as the event it stems from. But you are here. You and Shawn. And now you are holding hands, tightly. And you are talking to a reporter about being here, having come out on the other side of Amendment 2.

You are also thinking, if not talking, about having lived nearly thirty years of what will come to seem like another life. For that is the division that coming out makes, ultimately. Whether it speaks to the particularity, or granularity, or specificity, or even just the complex and messy truth about who you are (if that's a thing you can know, or that exists, as you remember that strange moment standing in your shower in 1993, believing you had no self, no real self, only demons coming in)—whatever it speaks to, coming out marks a division in your life, and your interview by a tv journalist in Colorado Springs in the summer of 1996 attests to that division, and in a way constitutes it.

What does that division mean? You'll spend a lot of time thinking about that—and just as much time thinking about the artificiality of said division (for there are so many aspects of what some might be tempted to consider your "former life" that you will hold on to, that won't be forgotten, that will not go quietly into a "before" that is separate or separable from your current "after"). The division will not explain that you could've stayed married, nor reconcile your complicated relationship to religious traditions, something you'll continue to work on. The division won't resolve the difficult legacies of abuse you suffered, the bullying that created a traumatic residue you'll find sprinkled throughout your life. Some narratives are through lines.

What has changed, dramatically, is how you are perceived by others in your immediate vicinity. Your interview, so brief, just thirty seconds, barely a cogent comment, will be seen by many in Pueblo, by friends and foes alike—foes you didn't even know you had. Foes you didn't have until this moment. You are now the "gay professor." You will discover death threats scribbled on bathroom walls. You will have rumors spread about you. You will supposedly be a menace to your students. You will not be welcome in some parts of town. You will have senior administrators attempt to keep you from advancing, from taking new positions, such as working as an advisor with new students. Yours will not be the face they want to put forward. Yours will not be the life they want to celebrate. At times, the hostility unleashed by this division will seem immediately threatening. You will be harassed on the streets of this very city, Colorado Springs, the city in which you celebrate your first Pride Day. On the flip side will be the gay guys who'll look at you a bit askance because you don't disavow the attractions your wife had for you, or the pleasures of vaginal intercourse. The straights who'll want you to conform to the "it was all a mistake" narrative when talking about your marriage. The bisexuals who'll want to know, when you ultimately settle down with a man, if that moves you from a Kinsey 3 to a Kinsey 6—just another old-fashioned, garden-variety homo. The trans folk, especially the younger ones, who'll see you increasingly as an aging gay who doesn't know anything about their lives, who likely only agreed to add the T to the LGB only to hide it under the banner of "queer."

Yes, there will be much to worry over within your supposed community in the coming years. Not just outside it. You will fight for that community just the same. You will stand in an election booth in the great state of Ohio, pulling a lever to vote against a city ordinance strikingly similar to Amendment 2, this time in the city of Cincinnati, where you and your husband will move from Colorado. A few years later, you'll stand in the same booth and vote for marriage equality. You'll win the first vote, lose the second. And you'll walk out of that booth both times and wonder: how many other people pulling those little levers today have actually voted on an issue that directly impacts their life?

Not long after, you'll rush your husband to the hospital for an emergency appendectomy, and you'll wait in the lounge while he's in surgery, for one hour, then two, then three. Mad with worry, you walk up to the nurses' station in the middle of the night to inquire after your . . . well, your not-exactly husband, since the voters of Ohio haven't extended your kind that right—and when you ask the nurse what's going on, she says, looking you straight in the face, "And just who exactly are you?" You lean in and say as softly and as forcefully as you can, knowing that this is your most menacing voice, "I'm the only one here asking." There's a beat, then she sits back and tells you everything is fine—and you still want to sue the crap out of this hospital, sue them into oblivion, and run screaming down the halls at the injustice of it all. And you think: *fuck all of these motherfuckers, fuck them all to hell for voting against us, for voting against our love, for trying to make our lives small, as small as their own fucking miserable lives.*

I don't want to take away from your moment, from the celebration, from your first Pride Day. I know part of you can intuit the challenges ahead. I also know part of you can't. That you have no idea what this dividing line will mean at the granular level in your life—but you know you've stepped over a line. The division is taking hold. Things will be different now.

"I Love You Always Forever"

DONNA LEWIS

And they are. You begin to question everything, asking yourself, *What am I doing here? Why am I still here?* Your job is okay; you enjoy your colleagues, you like your students, and you even find time to write. The pay is shit, though. You live month to month. And you suspect you'd find that time to write regardless, wherever you lived. So you think, *Could I have another life, a better life, someplace else?* The money and security aren't holding you back because, hey, they're pretty meager. But there's Karen. And Shawn. And then Shawn asks if you ever think of leaving. He wonders out loud, "Wouldn't it be interesting get out of here, set up shop someplace else? Where could we go?"

You're just sitting around on the floor of his bedroom, near the mattress you've been sucking his cock on, eating cheap pepperoni pizza and drinking cheap red wine out of plastic cups. And you start to wonder. To imagine. Wonder and imagine together. It feels . . . nice. Like you and Laura, years ago, speculating about the possibilities. *Where could we go? What could we do?* This time, though, you're wondering with a boy, a man, one who sometimes doubts the force and presence of his own beauty. But he is beautiful, especially in this moment, opening himself up, risking some imagination with you.

That emboldens you. You think, *What the fuck? Why not leave Pueblo?*

What have we got to lose? Perhaps you are motivated in part by fear—fear of living openly gay in a smallish town, just south of the home of Focus on the Family. Even in the aftermath of the overturning of Amendment 2, the place just doesn't feel completely . . . safe. Of course, no place ever will likely feel completely safe. But could there be somewhere that is *more* safe, whatever that might mean? You know the stories, the clichés, the small-town boys and girls and trans folk who move to the big cities, usually on the coasts, to pursue a more open life, a *safer* life. It's the story of Uncle Glen, moving to New Orleans, hoping to forget part of his past, lose himself in a community, however underground—a community of people relatively like him. It seemed to work, mostly. Could this, too, be your story? Might you be following in his footsteps, even if that's not consciously what you're thinking? But they *are* there, these thoughts, this sense that you might be repeating a pattern. And you find you're okay with that.

"What about Seattle?" Shawn says.

"Seattle. Yeah."

You're reminded, as soon as he says the name, that you and Laura honeymooned in Seattle. It wasn't much of a honeymoon. You'd both just graduated, and she had a job interview there. If she got the position, you'd gladly follow her, find something to do, apply to teach (which is what you ultimately did in Pueblo when the job in Seattle didn't come through). You were both excited. A big city. And on a coast!

These thoughts return to you, seeming like a path not taken, a trajectory denied, a possibility foreclosed upon. It's opening up again. It feels like a sign.

"Yeah, I could totally get behind Seattle."

"Cool, cool. I actually know a couple of people there. We could probably crash at their places while we figure things out, check out the job situation."

Just like that, moving to Seattle is more than a fantasy. It feels like an option, something you can see yourself doing with this man, this fellow young man, this lover. Yes, Shawn has become your lover. You tackle him from your seat on the floor, overturning your wine, and pin him to the bed, putting your weight on top of him, feeling his body, his mass, his shape, his muscles starting to writhe under his skin as he pretends to struggle. You pin his arms above his head and lean in to kiss him, pulling up, watching him smile, adoring that smile, that warmth. He's let you in. And now you're making plans to change everything.

"As I Lay Me Down"

SOPHIE B. HAWKINS

You're sitting outside a coffeeshop in Colorado Springs, talking with Shawn and an older woman, a friend of the family, Shawn's family, before they basically threw him out of the house for being queer. A middle-aged white woman, she's someone Shawn had gone to church with, someone who knew him as a child, who watched him grow and who, whatever her religious convictions, still chooses to love him, despite his family choosing differently.

She's skeptical about this Seattle plan.

"Are you sure about this? I mean, you don't really know this man," she offers, not unkindly, as she gestures toward me.

"But I do know him. We know exactly what we're doing."

She sips her coffee, raising an eyebrow, clearly biting back the words she wants to say next. It's not her life, not her decision. She knows this. She's raised her own children. She's said what she needed to say.

You all go for ice cream, and then Shawn and you go to the movies, and later that night, you suck his cock, he sucks your cock, and in the aftermath of your lovemaking, as you cuddle in dirty, sticky sheets, cum drying between you, you decide on a date to leave town.

"Let's take off in two weeks. Otherwise I don't think we'll do it."

"Totally. Two weeks."

"We're doing this. We're really fucking doing this."

"We are."

"Your eyes see through me."

"Shut up and let's fuck."

You both laugh and laugh, making out again before you fall asleep in each other's arms.

"Counting Blue Cars"

DISHWALLA

Shawn's roommates say they can easily find someone to take over his share of the large green Victorian on the corner near downtown, and your rent is month to month, so that part's easy. There are rounds of dinners and drinks with friends, an afternoon hanging out with just Karen, and even a visit to Laura to say goodbye. (Not only are you dating a Black guy, surprise surprise, so is she!)

Yes, you're doing it. You're going to Seattle. It's summer break, so you don't have to quit your job yet, but you don't exactly tell your department chair you won't be back in the fall. Prudence wins out. Why cut all ties so soon? This is, after all, something of an exploratory mission. Such caution almost feels like a leftover impulse from your life before, a way of playing it safe, of not counting your chickens, etc., though you're not thinking any of this consciously. You're too excited about "moving" to Seattle. With your lover. With your gay lover.

Shawn, though, turns in his notice at work. Perhaps he's more committed. Perhaps he's got less to lose. He hates the job at the bank. Some of the people are okay, but they're not enough of a reason to stay. They actually throw you both a going-away party. It's nice. A cheap cake and a bag of Doritos in the afternoon. A few tears, some possibly authentic. But Shawn is ready to go. Completely ready.

And then . . . you're off. You pack your car—a four-door Geo left over from your marriage, still on lease for the next two years—with some clothes, some books, and the desktop computer from your campus office. You're not exactly stealing it. You have every intention of returning it. (And yes, you take it knowing you'll have to bring it back, but in the moment you're thinking that will just be a visit, likely later this summer, so you can close out your life in Pueblo.) You reason that you need that computer because you intend to write in the coming weeks. You will not be giving that up. You have been writing regularly for years, even more so since your divorce. Short poems and fragments, bits and pieces, groping your way toward some as-yet-unseen whole.

A Friday afternoon in early July. Dry, but still hot. You'll be burning through gas with the air-conditioning, so you make a pact with Shawn: windows rolled down for as long as you both can stand, the air on sparingly. You need to conserve money. As is, you'll be paying for most of the trip because your salary continues through the summer, the compensation for nine months of teaching spread out thinly over twelve. So the race is on: get to Seattle, land jobs, start making money—start making a life—together, away. The clock is ticking.

You drive north, through Denver, stopping overnight—only a hundred miles north of Pueblo—to visit with some of Shawn's friends. They express a wondrous skepticism: *are you sure you know what you're doing? You actually quit your job? Sounds crazy, but okay, good luck!* After a cheap dinner at a taco stand, you all find yourselves at a dance club—gay, of course—pounding the floor to Alanis Morissette's "You Oughta Know." And *pounding* is the word. You oughta know. You should've known. You should've known so many, many things . . . that the boys you loved wouldn't love you back, not Matt, not Ethan . . . that the crushes were going to leave you completely unfulfilled. Like Alanis, you turn what you should've known into what they should know now—that you don't need them, that you're fine, that you're onto them and their lack of generosity, their disdain for you, their privileged straight selfish bullshit, and so fuck them, fuck them all. You and your lover are moving to Seattle. You oughta know.

The next morning, not exactly hungover but a little tired, you're off again, headed toward Cheyenne. Lunch at a Denny's, because it's cheap. Then across southern Wyoming, past Laramie, where later this decade a young man named Matthew Shepard will be tricked, robbed, beaten, and left for dead, nearly crucifix style, on the open prairie. Others like him have certainly been attacked and even killed, regularly, for quite some time, but the national outrage is yet to come, and your hearts are light as you drive along this desolate road, quickly becoming more and more like a moonscape, abandoned, lifeless, looking forward to your new life, just not here. As you cross the continental divide and snake into a corner of Utah, weariness creeps up on you. It grows late, and without realizing it, you start to nod off—Shawn asleep to your side, your head drooping, lolling . . . and then your body jerks and you look up, realizing you've been driving while not fully conscious. You wake Shawn so he can help you find a KOA.

In the dark, you both pitch a tent, a wedding gift (you've forgotten from whom) that you and Laura used a couple of times, camping in the Alabama woods in the fall. You loved it. You wish you'd camped more. You will now, to save money. And it's nice. Cool at night. You cuddle together, too tired for sex but glad for each other's warmth in this high country.

It's nearly 10 when you wake and pack up, looking for some kind of coffee before you get too far. Once you're out of Utah, you move into Idaho, where you'll stop again before heading westward toward Oregon, making a beeline to Portland and then straight north to Seattle. Your third day, you're relaxing into the trip, the steady thrumming of the car, the miles lapped up, the sheer beauty of the landscape. It's all so fucking gorgeous. The grandeur. Natural spectacle. All spread out before you. The wide open road. The wide open West. Go west, young man. And indeed, you are.

You press on to Boise, which is surprisingly cute, and you both decide to stop for a while. Yes, this is Idaho, where Mark Furhman moved in the aftermath of the O. J. Simpson trial, a state apparently full of conservative militia, not exactly screaming "gay friendly." But you're nonetheless charmed, both of you, by Boise. Maybe it reminds you of the town you've just left, snuggled up against the mountains. It certainly has some good coffee shops, with baristas who tell you what's cool to see, like a funky little museum of "modern art" that's mostly just abstracts of lonesome cowboys. But hey, something, at least. You just need to be out of the car, as fun as the drive has been. You decide to go to the movies, check out *Independence Day*, the updated *War of the Worlds*, which turns out to be a jingoistic bit of US propaganda. *America saves the world, yet again, from invasion. America to the galactic rescue!* You're both a little outraged, sitting in the packed theater—what fucking hubris this country has! And oh yeah, it's the Fourth of July. Funny how you'd almost forgotten, so set are you both on your own independence.

Instead of looking for a place to camp, you splurge on a Motel 6, showering together and then flopping on the bed, pleasantly tired, and a little aroused now that you've had a break from the perpetual motion of the car. You reach into your bag near the nightstand and pull out a pair of metal handcuffs you bought at an army surplus store in Colorado Springs. Shawn smiles as you straddle him, pinning his wrists above his head with one hand and slapping on the cuffs with the other. Having secured him, you roughly flip him over and spank his ass, delivering several tough slaps as he grinds his crotch into the mattress. You flip him again and kiss him deeply before coming up for air.

"You're so fucking hot."

You've never heard those words before—not about you, not spoken in the midst of a sexual act. You plunge back into his mouth, then snake your tongue down his chin, his chest, his bellybutton, and then swallow his cock until he's humping your mouth, pumping his hips into your face, his hands still cuffed above his head.

"Time"

HOOTIE & THE BLOWFISH

In the morning, you're back in the car, heading west across Oregon until you finally hit Portland. You stop for an early dinner and a roam through the downtown area, hitting up the famous bookstore, Powell's, a place you'll find yourself returning to again and again in the years to come, a "safe space," a sacred space, a shrine to the one thing that has seemed so constant in your life—the pleasure, the joy, the ecstasy of reading. No matter what else has happened, no matter how your various loves and desires and relationships have formed, deformed, fluctuated, and faltered, you have had books. Seeing this massive bookstore, occupying an entire city block and extending upwards four stories, seeing this monument to reading seems like a sign—you are on the right path. Indeed, all of Portland seems that way. The clouds and light summer rain, the young people everywhere, the ubiquitous coffee, the gray smudge of grunge—all of this feels like a foretaste of Seattle. You are getting closer, oh so much closer.

Back in the car, you head north. You're just a couple of hours away, then an hour. Finally you crest a large hill and see the city laid out in the distance, the spires, the Space Needle prominent amongst them, and you could almost cry. You don't, but Shawn reaches out to hold your hand as you drive down the hill into the future.

"Shawn, tell me all your thoughts on god."

You're quoting a song on the radio, something you've heard a few times over the last thousand miles, but you're both too tired for conversation, nor do you feel like camping in the chilly drizzle. You find another Motel 6 for the night, and the next day, Shawn calls his friend, the woman who works in tech up here, like many other young people. She lives way on the other side of the city, and it takes over an hour to get to her place—a cookie-cutter subdivision, a featureless beige condo. But this will do. You at least don't have to pay for it. The friend, Shelly, is reserved. You wonder how close she and Shawn really are, but you're not asking too many questions. It's a place to stay.

Shelly works at an office and is gone before you wake up. You hope she's not avoiding you both but push the thought aside as you spend the day exploring. You recognize some things from your honeymoon with Laura, but you don't really know the layout of the city, so oddly the experience seems both comfortable and fresh. You have been here before, but you've also built this place up in your dreams as somewhere you might live more freely. It will take some time to disappoint, and in the end, you won't know if the city has failed you or if your dream has. But you're getting ahead of yourself. There's so much to see and do. Coffee everywhere. Fresh fish. Beautiful young people. You spend most of your time in Capitol Hill, where all the gays are. Rainbow flags everywhere. Cute boys. Butch girls. Nothing like this in Colorado outside of a square block or two of Denver. And it isn't even Pride! You're feeling good about this. You smile a lot. You and Shawn hold hands, feeling at home already.

You even check out a one-bedroom apartment that's only $400 a month! A bit cramped, but it's right in the middle of Capitol Hill, so you'd likely not be spending much time in it. Still, you start thinking the rent is nearly half your current income, which reminds you that your current income only lasts another couple of months. And then what? You settle in with Shawn at a coffeeshop to talk about reality. What are you both going to do for cash? How will this work? You find a local newspaper and start looking through the ads, at least to give you some ideas. Ah, you see something, something you hadn't thought of before: elderly caregiver. You could totally do that. You worry you'd have to downplay your education, not mention you have a PhD. But that's okay. It's a job, not a career. You both head to the social services office and fill out an application. You've done something for the day, taken a step forward. You give Shelly's phone number as the contact and hope she won't mind. After all, it means you're that much closer to getting out of her living room, off her futon.

Then Shawn has another idea. He was involved in environmental activism during college and remembers that Ralph Nader established a nationwide group of largely college-based activists. Why not check out a local branch and see if they need help—paid help? It's an inspired thought; you like the progressive-mindedness of it. So sure! And you both hit paydirt. They do need people, and they're willing to pay you to go door-to-door in the Seattle suburbs, looking for donations. You can start right away! Tomorrow! You're initially charmed by the offer, but as you walk away with your packet of information, you have your first misgiving. You might be willing to downplay your credentials so you can do elder care, washing and reading to old folks, changing sheets, perhaps even a diaper or two, but did you really get a PhD so you could beg strangers for money? Yes, yes, the cause is right—environmental justice is so important—but your enthusiasm falters over the course of the day. Shawn, though, is ecstatic. He knows these people. He's worked with them before. He feels great about the possibilities. He sees himself moving up in the organization. His dream unfurls, and in the morning he bounds out of bed to get dressed and go ask for money.

You get up and start to make coffee but stop because something feels off. You don't know what it is at first, but the feeling gets worse. You can't breathe. You feel like you're suffocating. Tears come to your eyes. You can't stand up straight. *You're having a panic attack.*

"What's wrong, oh my god, what's wrong? Do we need to call an ambulance?"

"No, no, no, I'm okay," you mumble between gasps.

"You're scaring the crap out of me!"

"I know, I know." You sit down, and your breathing starts to slow. You inhale deeply and wipe a tear from your eye. "I don't want to go with you on the donation run."

Shawn pauses, his face blank. "Okay . . . ?"

"I'm sorry, but I don't think it's for me."

Shawn doesn't know what to say, so he says the only thing he can. "Don't worry about it. You stay here. I'll take the car, and you can just rest. Read. Make some coffee. Watch tv. It'll be okay."

You're not so sure.

That evening, Shawn comes back and has had a good time. It's tough work, but he believes in it. You begin to wonder: what do you believe in? You've spent the day reading, thinking, reading, napping. You're calmer. Calm enough that, after a quick run for a burger, you think you'll make it up to Shawn by giving him a blowjob. Yeah, a nice gesture. He steps out for a cigarette after dinner, something he doesn't do often but feels like tonight, after a day pounding pavement. He comes back in, undresses, settles in next to you, and you cuddle, his back to your front. You make your move, turning him over to face you so you can kiss him. He opens his mouth, you go in, then you pull back in involuntary disgust.

"Fuck, your mouth tastes like an ashtray." You can't help yourself. It just comes out.

"I forgot to gargle, sorry," he offers, hurt, turning away.

Fuck, you think. *Just fuck.* In a half hour, his back to you, he's snoring. *Fuck.*

"Don't Cry"

SEAL

The next morning, Shawn decides he doesn't want to go in to work. You've been at Shelly's a couple of nights, and you really need to find another place. She's leaving early and coming home late, clearly avoiding you both. You've overstayed your welcome. So you pack the car and head back into town. Camping is out of the question; it's just too fucking wet. Maybe a youth hostel? It would be cheaper than a Motel 6. And you could meet some people, maybe some people with ideas for work or leads on other places to live.

The chilliness outside the car, even in a Seattle summer, matches the chilliness inside it. Something has shifted. Your moods improve a little when you find a cybercafe in Capitol Hill and can search for a hostel, Shawn on one computer, you on another. You splurge on a mocha; Shawn declines your offer to buy him a coffee. When you check your email, there's something from Bill, the chair of your department back in Pueblo: "Hi, just wanted to see how you're doing. Also wondering if you plan to come back in the fall. If not, we need to find someone to teach your courses. Of course, we'd love to have you back."

Now something in *you* shifts. Decidedly. You realize that, whatever drawbacks might lie in Colorado, your friends are there, your job is there—and it's a job you actually love. Yes, there are frustrations. And you're going to have to teach, for the first time, with everyone knowing that you're a gay man, an openly gay man. It won't be easy. You know there will be comments, insinuations. It could really suck. But it might very damn well be incredible. You don't know, though that *might* seems more of a promise for the future than you have here. You want to go home.

Home . . . the word surprises you. Of course, you're away from everything you know, tired of being itinerant in a strange—and very wet—city. And also increasingly wondering about you and Shawn. He wants to leave Colorado behind, but you're beginning to think—and feel—that you're not done there yet. That maybe, having come out, having staked your claim to an identity, you need to see how that plays out in the place you've started to build a life. You still get the allure of the radically different and oh-so-urban Seattle, and Capitol Hill's rainbow pride is certainly attractive. But perhaps this isn't the right time. You need a job. Preferably one you want to do, one you value. And you do value teaching, connecting with young people.

The hostel found, you both head to it, unpack your bags, stretch out on the lumpy bed. You snagged a semiprivate room; you only have to share the bath. It's turned out to be a beautiful day, the drizzle subsiding, the sun shining, the winds calm. You lie side by side, looking out the window. Silent. You take a breath.

"Bill emailed me."

"Oh?"

"He wants to know if I'm teaching in the fall."

A beat. Two.

"What did you tell him?"

"I haven't replied yet."

Another beat.

"You want to go back."

"I do."

Shawn rolls over, away from you. He can't make it here on his own. Only you have income for the next couple of months, and precious little but still something saved up in your bank account. You're calling the shots, and Shawn knows it, which is why you couldn't say out loud that you want to go back. You made him say it. It's not fair.

None of it ever is.

"Breakfast at Tiffany's"

DEEP BLUE SOMETHING

You both decide to spend a couple more days in Seattle, just exploring, enjoying. Bill gets your email and is pleased you'll be returning; it's less work for him, after all. No need to find replacements for your four courses. Still, you clock his reply as a sign that you're wanted, or at least needed to make life less of a hassle. You'll take it.

Shelly ends up meeting you in Capitol Hill for brunch. She seems warmer, likely because you're both out of her condo. You treat her to thank her for her hospitality. She and Shawn chat, and she blinks when Shawn rolls his eyes a bit and tells her you've decided to go back. To his credit, he's been a trouper about this, not questioning your decision, not even really complaining—until now. You've soothed your conscience by thinking—even suggesting—that he can likely go back to the bank. He's not impressed. He hated that job. But what choice does he have?

Walking down the street after brunch, headed toward a bookstore or two, you offer an olive branch: "I bet I can get my old apartment back. You're welcome to move in with me. . . ."

"Let's not make any plans, okay? No promises."

You can't blame him, but it still stings.

"Mouth"

MERRIL BAINBRIDGE

Two days later, you're packed up and back in the car. You don't have much more than when you left a couple weeks ago. Maybe a few extra books. And some resentments building, on both sides. You keep yours relatively to yourself, and so does he.

To do something different, you decide not to bypass Utah this time and instead head toward Salt Lake City, driving through the salt flats—which are extraordinary. All of Utah is gorgeous, stunning. Bright and clear, mountains surrounding you, the salt flats a seemingly endless expanse of white on both sides of the blacktopped highway. So alien, so otherworldly.

In Salt Lake, after you check in to the Motel 6, you tour the Mormon Temple grounds, because why the hell not? Following along with the group, you whisper to each other about how creepy it all is. Then, at the end of the tour, after a video about Joseph Smith and his trek to Utah to set up the Mormon utopia—Mormonland, the locals call it—the guide, a pretty young woman, earnestly asks the gathered visitors if they are ready to cease their wandering in the desert and come home: "The Church is waiting for you, with open arms."

You both leave quickly. It's too weird. By now you know what promises to turn away from. You also know better what promises not to make, not to make too soon.

You find a coffee shop and sit with your mochas in some cushy seats, across from two young women with multiple ear piercings, dyed hair, grungy clothes. You take a chance, lean in.

"Hi, we're just passing through and were wondering if there's a gay part of town?"

The women pause to look at each other, then look back at you. "You're sitting in it."

"Okay, thanks."

Back at the motel, having eaten your fast-food burgers, you lounge in front of the television, side by side on the bed. When Shawn reaches over and starts to fondle you, you're surprised. You didn't think that sex was on the agenda now. No promises, after all.

"Let's just have some fun, okay?"

And you do—but you leave the handcuffs in your bag, the rough-housing in your head.

No promises.

"Wonder"

NATALIE MERCHANT

You aren't yet aware of how you are transgressing one of the major narratives of "coming out," of how you are leaving behind the "big city"—to which, admittedly, you had flown, "escaping" rural Southern Colorado, and by extension the rurality of your youth in the Deep South—and are now returning to the small town, a place where things might not be easy for you as an openly gay person, not as easy as they would be if you lived in Capitol Hill. This detour, at least at this point, is driven by economic need, no doubt. But perhaps also by a sense that you don't want to flee. Not anymore. Leaving Louisiana and your family, and even getting married (which facilitated that flight, giving you a partner in escape)—all of that has been important to you. But it's time to stop running . . . to stop running away.

Your future self will piece together this narrative, your narrative, though it may not be true to what you experience at the time, driving back through wastelands and mountains—but even at the tender age of twenty-eight, you know that many things can be true at the same time, even things that don't seem like they should be. You will write about that, imagining a mother baking cookies for your college lover, who is of course a version of Mike, and maybe also a version of Matt, who was never a lover—a version of both of them, and neither of them. You will experience the simultaneity of truth and untruth, the truth that exists in the not-quite-true, when your future husband wonders why your mother gave this lover cookies when she's never done the same for him. But of course, there were no cookies. And then, suddenly, suddenly, there are. For your mother will, long after your father dies, move in with you and your husband, and she'll bake many cookies. Too many cookies. You future self will have to tell her to stop. Far too much sugar, and too much butter, especially when you and your husband decide to go vegan.

I'm getting ahead of myself, ahead of you, again. It's what we do. Like taking off for Seattle with a young man you've just met. Then, conversely, perversely, backtracking, retreading, but (hopefully) not repeating. You will hold on to this time with Shawn, however it's now ending, as an important move, more than a gesture; a way of taking a chance, a risk—something you won't frequently do, but something you will want to know that you *can* do.

Back in Pueblo, Shawn's roommates haven't given his room away just yet, and he says you can stay with him until you get your own place.

When you wake that first morning, having gotten in late and crashed, the space next to you is empty. You wonder if Shawn moved at some point in the night, wanting to sleep apart. There's a little nugget of pain somewhere inside, but it doesn't prevent you from quickly showering, getting dressed, and heading to campus. You want to get the computer out of your car and back in your office before anyone notices it's gone. While hooking up the machine and shelving your new books, you go over your time in Seattle. You hold a paperback you bought and think of the cybercafe, the hostel, handcuffing Shawn. The ringing phone interrupts you.

"Hey, where'd you go?"

"Hey. I came to my office to put the computer away. Where'd you go?"

"I couldn't sleep. I made you coffee, but you'd already gone."

"Ah, sorry."

"It's okay. See you tonight?"

"Yeah. See you tonight."

You hang up, touched. You then call Karen, and she meets you for lunch. After your burger at the student center, you both walk around campus, largely deserted for the summer.

You tell Karen everything, then talk about what's happened in Pueblo since you left. Karen wants to know if you and Shawn will move in together. You shake your head.

"I'm sorry."

"Don't be."

You smile, she smiles, and you know you will be friends for a very long time. All these years later, you still are.

The mountains in the distance, Pikes Peak, the Sangre de Cristo, have no snow on their tops in the warm months, but there's a good wind, steady, coming from the west. You lift your head to it and breathe.

Acknowledgments

Any book is the work of numerous folks, even if they don't always know they've been involved. In the case of *Dear Queer Self*, some of my debts are obvious. First and foremost, Nicola Mason, editor of Acre Books, took a chance on this book, and I will be forever grateful. Eileen Joy and Vincent W. J. van Gerven Oei got me started publishing book-length creative nonfiction, and Tom Lutz and Boris Dralyuk encouraged the habit. So too did Michelle Latiolais, and I hope she never regrets it. More personally, Karen Yescavage, David Lumb, Susan Jarratt, Sherryl Vint, George Lang, Nasrin Rahimieh, Robin Buck, David Wallace, Cristina and Tim Garrity have been the family I've needed to help me do this work. And, of course, Mack McCoy and Sophie Alexander and Cooper—what would I be without you?

Nicola will appreciate how much I've been thinking of James Olney as I've watched this book come together. James directed my doctoral studies at Louisiana State University a long time ago. He also mentored and was close friends with the writer Michael Griffith, Nicola's husband and my former classmate at LSU, and later my colleague at the University of Cincinnati. I know we all miss James. And little did I know that his long-term interest in autobiography, which I ignored when I studied with him, would plant a seed in my life. I am grateful in ways I never knew I could be. If this book had a dedicatee, it would be James Olney. And with that, so shall it be.